Testament of a R·

BOOKS BY

W. R. LOADER

No Joy of Africa
The Guinea Stamp
Through a Dark Wood
Staying the Distance
Testament of a Runner

Books written under the pseudonym of

DANIEL NASH

My Son is in the Mountains
Not Yours the Island
The Lovely Crew
Stay the Execution
A Hero's Welcome

Testament of a Runner

W. R. LOADER

THE KINGSWOOD PRESS

For my
FATHER

The Kingswood Press
an imprint of William Heinemann Ltd
10 Upper Grosvenor Street, London W1X 9PA

LONDON MELBOURNE
JOHANNESBURG AUCKLAND

Copyright © W. R. Loader 1960

First published 1960 by William Heinemann Ltd in association
with The Naldrett Press Ltd
Reprinted 1987 by The Kingswood Press
ISBN 0 434 98106 0

Printed and bound in Great Britain by
Biddles Ltd, Guildford and King's Lynn

FOREWORD

BOOKS ON SPORT occupy only the foothills of literature. The subject is, by its very nature, too restricted, its scope too lacking in universal relevance to scale the pinnacles. Yet, among these foothills, *Testament of a Runner* is a beacon of excellence. Few books in this century have captured the essential *espirit* of sport with the same graphic intensity.

When it was first published in 1960 it was acclaimed with delight by athletes who found, perhaps for the first time, a literary echo of their own concerns and aspirations. When I returned to it 20 years later, while preparing to run in the London Marathon, I found renewed and germane delight in its articulation of the runner's faith. As a result I urged the publisher to reprint the book now that there is a far greater interest in athletics than there was 20 years ago. It would surely fulfil the yearnings of expression for the new generation of joggers and mass marathons, as *Chariots of Fire* had done on film. Fortunately, the publisher responded, and now this new generation will be able to respond in turn to Bill Loader's self-revelations which speak to every athlete, whether Olympic champion or humble twice-round-the-park-before-breakfast jogger.

This book was a pioneer in sporting books. It set new standards. Until its publication, books on sport were rarely of quality, although there were some obvious exceptions like the works of Cardus in cricket, or Roger Bannister's *The First Four Minutes*.

Most of the successors of *Testament of a Runner*, however, dealt only with outstanding contemporary performers. What makes this book remarkable is that it deals with both a little-known athlete, and also with an earlier period in time. Even in 1960, the 1920s and 1930s seemed distant. Now they seem archaic. Did athletes really run with cork grips strapped to their hands with elastic rings to ensure the fist was closed? Yet, part of the pleasure of the book is the recreation of the atmosphere of a forgotten era of athletics and its description of the people who provided its very fabric: men like George Eliot, who refused to give up when his foot had been broken, ('Oh, aye the foot is jibbing a bit. But if a chap stopped running every time he got a bit ache or pain, then he'd never run at all would he?'); Paddy Blane ('Some spring inside the man had been wound up and never seemed to wind down'); Bunghole, with his search for the perfect laxative; Dimitri, the Greek, who advocated drinking oil to improve performance; and Spuggy, the schoolmaster, whose lack of evident enthusiasm for Loader's performance served only to goad him on still further towards the AAA Junior 100 yards title.

But *Testament of a Runner* particularly works because its central theme is the spirit of an athlete: the enduring questions of why he competes and exercises, the anxiety before an event, the pleasure to be gained from moving fast, and the struggle between conscience and reason in a training session. Loader expresses this well because of his personal experience of running, enabling him to recognise its special conflicts. He conveys his own preoccupations in an unusually direct manner. He is truthful to himself. There is a constant tension in the telling because it is informed by the complete biographical experience with all its varying emotions, experiences and worries.

If, like *Chariots of Fire*, the book occasionally veers towards schoolboy sentimentality and triteness, it is usually saved by this honesty with the reader, the recognition of his own complex feelings about the activity. Loader does not indulge himself – a constant trap in any writing, and especially with an auto-biography. His frankness engages the reader as he questions the mentality and motives. The runner, he concludes, is an egoist, but he suffers for it.

'Science' he writes, 'can tell us something of a fact already known, but doesn't make a big contribution towards discovering the ultimate "why"'. *Testament of a Runner* may not give us the answer, but perhaps more than any other book on sport it addresses itself to the question.

John Goodbody
Sports News Correspondent
The Times
September, 1986

CHAPTER ONE

JACK LONDON was the first man I ever saw run. I mean, really run. The distinction may seem a fine one, and was certainly not appreciated by many people in the north-east coast town where I lived as a boy. Even among the professed sprinters, men who fancied themselves as quick movers and were so fancied by others, there were those who seemed to regard running as a base, mechanic exercise, a means of progressing from point A to point B convenient for a person who couldn't afford to take a taxi. That puts far too low an estimation on running. One might equally regard 'The Bluebells of Scotland', laboriously picked out by a child preparing for the first examination in music, as the ultimate in piano-playing.

Running is not an affair of applied mechanics or economic necessity but an expression by the human body of rhythm and grace and strength which, at its best, rises above the immediate and practical requirements of a given race. If you define poetry as the right words in the right order, then good running is the right movements in the right tempo. Perfection of control is to be seen in it, and a nice economy of effort, and a sense of man's physical potentiality being fulfilled and completed. Much has been said and written of the beauty of motion as observed in animals, little of that same beauty when man is the mover. No one, as I passed from childhood to boyhood, had spoken to me about it in terms that I could understand, and the few local runners whom I had seen in action gave no cause for the conception of such an idea. On a mind unprepared for the vision, the sight of Jack London sprinting struck like a lightning flash.

A group of us had entered for the 80 yards boys' race at the local Police Sports. We were all under twelve, and all nervous, having had no previous experience of public competition. Our mothers had rigged us out in a colourful and unorthodox array of running kit, nearly all of it home-made and designed to impress the onlookers with maternal sewing skill rather than to give the wearers maximum freedom of movement. Football jerseys and flannel shirts, white or grey, clothed our torsoes, while our lower halves were encased in football shorts or voluminous, flapping linen drawers. One child stood aloof from the rest of us, in an agony of shame and despair, having been issued with what looked like a pair of his sister's navy-blue bloomers. Several urchins kept their school caps on. They evidently calculated, with justice, that the speed of their passage through the air wouldn't create enough wind to blow them off.

Our surroundings were utterly alien to us. Everything in them conspired to terrify junior schoolboys whose athletics efforts hitherto had been made against known quantities in the cosy, familiar world of school or neighbourhood recreation ground. Here nothing was known or cosy or familiar. We viewed the stadium of our town's Third Division football club with the same apprehension that an early Christian must have felt when he saw the Colosseum. No lions could actually be seen, but occasionally, above the brassy music of the military band, we seemed to detect an angry roar. Each other we viewed furtively, with scarcely less apprehension. The boys around us were strangers. They looked so much bigger and more powerful and more confident than we did ourselves. It must have been lunacy that prompted the desire to prove ourselves in competition

2

against them. Who were we to prove ourselves in competition against anybody, anywhere?

They had parted us from our parents, who looked even more anxious about our prospects than we did, and put us in a small tent by ourselves to change. The light in the tent was sombre and greenish, which fitted very well the prevailing mood. Self-conscious and for the most part silent we undressed, draping our outdoor clothes across the grim, iron-framed wooden benches that lined the walls of the tent.

'Yah, bloomers!' someone muttered to the shame-faced wretch who had struggled into the garment with elasticated legs, but the insult was half-hearted, with no real bite to it.

Opposite stood the marquee where the men stripped. Odours of wintergreen and embrocation drifted across from it. Unseemly words were uttered as a bare foot trod on an upturned pair of spiked shoes. Somewhere inside that marquee was Jack London, the big name, the legendary figure coaxed down from Olympus by the meeting organisers to draw the crowds. It awed us that a demigod could be presented on the same programme as a bunch of schoolchildren. Only a week or two previously had London returned from the Olympic Games at Amsterdam, where he took second place for Britain in the 100 metres. During a heat he equalled the then Olympic record for the distance of 10.6 seconds. Forgotten now, J. E. London was a world-class sprinter of his day.

Long before our time of trial was due we were ready. Miserably, with clammy hands, we gathered near the tent door and gazed out upon the arena. As yet there were no blood-stains on the grass. The hundred yards track – to be cut short by twenty yards for our benefit – was marked out not with chalked lines but in the old style with tapes stretched about a foot from the ground through long

3

skewer-like pegs. At one end of the track the white-coated starter tested his guns. The reports made us jump. Blue smoke curled away from the muzzles, and bits of paper wadding from the expended blank cartridges fell gently through the still air. The ranks of spectators were thickening in the stands. Gleaming silver cups winked and flashed on the prize table. The military band played a heartlessly jaunty air. My knees were made of jelly. I couldn't stop myself yawning. With all my heart I wished I had never asked to face this ordeal. Suddenly a steward put his head round the tent door.

'Competitors for the scholars' race!' he shouted. 'All out, boys!'

Green-faced and shivering one boy went into a corner and got rid of the high tea which he had rashly eaten. Another child, the one wearing his sister's bloomers, burst into tears. The rest of us trailed into the open with all the gaiety of candidates for Tyburn Tree.

About other branches of athletics I might not be so dogmatic, but about sprinting I would say that you either are a sprinter, or you aren't. You can't make yourself a sprinter by taking thought, any more than you can add a cubit to your stature. There must be physical ability, but even more important there must be mental drive. The physical ability may be developed by training and the mental drive may be sharpened by knowledge, but if the drive isn't present in the first place no one is ever going to put it there.

This is something more easily seen than explained. They used to say of J. Donaldson, the great Australian professional who dominated pedestrianism in the years before the First World War, that he ran like a wild dingo in anxious pursuit of its prey. The man couldn't have been anything else but a sprinter. You recognised the fact at once, as soon as he began to go down the track. So reluctant

4

did he seem to remain in contact with the ground that it might have been a bed of hot coals that he was traversing. His whole mind and body were devoted to the task of hurling himself in the direction of the tape. He was one of Nature's fast movers.

It is possible to be one of Nature's fast movers, and yet not realise it. The mental fuse may be laid at an early age, but the question is, when will a match be put to it. Watch any group of young schoolboys running. Most of them trundle along like sheep escaping rather half-heartedly from the not very terrifying presence of a Pekinese dog. There is no urgency in their movements, no sense of the tap being turned full on. Instead of keeping their eyes fixed on the finish they're glancing sideways at their competitors. They may even slow up to make sure they don't get too far away from the comfort of the flock.

But every now and then you will see a youngster who goes with drive and determination, running as if a hot iron were touching his backside, desperate not only to be first, but to be first by a hell of a long way. At some stage in his life he has discovered the fierce joy that comes from moving at speed, from putting every ounce of strength and nervous energy into the business of propelling his body forward. That youngster is a sprinter. He knows that he can go faster than his fellows, he wants to go faster than his fellows. But the important thing is that he not only runs fast against opponents. He gets an almost equal joy from running fast against himself.

The true point of departure in the career of a sprinter is the time when he first feels his behind being touched by the hot iron. In my case the vision of Jack London and the scorching coincided. A by-product of the affair was the winning of a small leather attaché case, valued on the programme at twelve shillings and sixpence. If justice were done, this ought to have been presented to London. He won the race in the spirit, even if I went through the tape in the flesh. But doubtless he would have waived his claim to the trophy had the matter been put to him.

We clustered near the start, not looking as if this were the happiest moment in our lives. In one way it was good not to be in the first heats, since we had a chance of seeing what the correct procedure was in this solemn affair. In another way it was bad, for the sight of others undergoing their ordeal sharpened the fears at the thought of our own. The starter's gun thundered like a cannon. Instead of leaping forward at the sound, some of the boys recoiled backwards, or got tangled in the tapes. The front markers who did this wrought havoc among the back markers. I was a back marker. The thought of having to bull-doze a path through a bunch of lurching opponents before the race could even be started did not appeal. Not only my knees were jelly now, but also my bowels.

'Heat 4!' the starter's marksman shouted.

Oh, misery, the time had come. They were urging us forward, like lambs into slaughterhouse pens. The spectators were watching with a cruel, light-hearted detachment. They had even laughed when one poor devil in heat 3 tripped over shoes that were too big for him and nose-dived into the turf. Laughed at a tragedy! Laughter was worse than the roar of lions. At all costs, no cause for laughter must be given. Everything seemed big and overwhelming – the concrete stands, the expanse of the grassy pitch, the officials around us, the track which seemed so long that it narrowed away in the distance like railway lines. We felt small and weak in the face of this hugeness. No doubt there are many runners who have made their first public appearance in such a contest and who, on looking back, understand that this was the first humble rung of a ladder which

6

eventually led up to modest success in the world of athletics.

But at the time you don't realise that this is the foot of a ladder you're approaching. It seems more like the top of a cliff. Yet you still go blindly forward. All you're conscious of is that you have to run in this heat of the scholars' race for under-twelves if it's the last thing you do: that the starter's marksman is shouting at you impatiently because you've taken the wrong position on the grid: that your heart is beating somewhere high up in your throat: and that you're terrified in case the elastic waistband of your home-made shorts should snap halfway through the race and thus expose you to the mockery of the watching throng.

The elastic didn't snap. Nobody slumped forward at the report of the gun, blood-stains spreading direly across grey flannel shirt. (They had assured us that a live round couldn't possibly get mixed up with the blank, but we didn't believe them.) Everyone got away, and in a forward direction, without fouling the tapes which demarcated the lanes. Judged by the standards that could be expected to apply to us, it was a good start.

But it was a poor race, even though I won it.

In a great arena and on an occasion so important I had vaguely expected even junior schoolboys' running, by some strange alchemy, to be lifted to a higher plane, to be more vital and gripping than a clumsy playground canter. It was precisely to get away from the ruck of playground canters that I had entered for this event. Here we were, competing for a real prize, in front of spectators who had actually paid to get into the stadium. Our names were printed in the programme. The sports promoters had sent us numbers, as well as safety-pins with which to affix them to our shirts or jerseys. For us, admission was free. A tent had been placed at our sole disposal. Despite the crowd's indulgent laughter at the antics of schoolboys the occasion had a solemnity and formality about it to which we should have responded with some inspired running. We didn't. At the start we all showed the same old hesitancy, though that was partly due to rubber-soled gym shoes slipping on juicy grass. When we got going our arm and leg movements were clumsy and ill-co-ordinated. In full flight our progress was the galumphing trot of a man floundering through treacle. I only won the heat because some little idiot checked a yard from the finish – a typical schoolboy error, this – and let me through.

To reach the final was satisfactory, but not to reach it in such an untidy, scrambling way. What should have been a sword thrust turned out to be no more than a shaky prod with a rag doll. Walking away from the finish I shook my head. This wasn't running, not the sort of running that grown-ups talked about in terms of such excitement, even of wonder. When men spoke of Donaldson or Applegarth or Paddock or London they made them sound like heroes, giants, creatures whose sprinting was a flash of flame and not a dull, earth-bound movement. A boy could not expect to be a hero, but surely, if he hoped eventually to become even a pale reflection of these great names, there should be an early revelation of his quality? Did a runner, a real runner, have some ingredient in his make-up that other people didn't possess? If so, what was it? Merely the difference in strength between a man and a boy, or something beyond that? Would some secret be revealed in the fullness of time, like other secrets that grown-ups fought shy of revealing to us? Would one learn the secret this evening?

An interval separated the heats and final of the scholars' race. During the interval the main business of the evening began. Already the competitors had come out for the two-lap Novices cycle race. Between the skeleton crash helmets and the bright club jerseys their faces looked pale and apprehensive. The sudden interest taken in the proceedings by the ambulance men did nothing to lessen their apprehension. Interest among the crowd stirred. The thick, juicy grass was in good shape to cause a front wheel skid, which might be followed by a tangle of lightweight bicycles and a gashed leg or two. No one actually hoped for a spill, but an accident certainly lent colour and drama to a race. Expectantly the ambulance men got their stretchers ready, and checked the iodine and sal volatile and bandages in their haversacks. Terrified by these preparations, the novices proceeded with such extreme caution on their mounts that a good half-miler could probably have covered the distance on foot in a faster time.

'Ye've forgotten to take the brakes off, lad!' someone in the crowd shouted to the leader, well aware that racing machines have no brakes.

'Careful, hinny, or ye'll wear the tyres oot,' another voice advised.

Sullen and abashed under the jeering the novices got through their preliminaries, and gave way to the heats of the men's 100 yards flat handicap.

As usual, this event had attracted a big field. Men wearing the colours of all the clubs in the district pranced over the grass. No one paid them much attention. Interest was mainly focused on a tall, lean, brown-skinned man whose vest was white with two narrow hoops, one red and one blue, circling the midriff. Jack London moved easily round the track, looking not so very different from an ordinary human being. But no ordinary human being would have had his name in such big letters on the placards posted outside the stadium. And no ordinary human being could have caused the bustle of excitement that passed through the crowd like a breeze rippling a cornfield. Not often did

9

the north-east of England get the chance of seeing a runner of London's calibre in action. He made the crowd feel that they were in touch with the big world outside. Here was a man who'd beaten the magic figure of 'level time' for the hundred. Could he beat it tonight? Could he even get down to 10 seconds, which would be a good enough achievement on this track? Would some local athlete spring a surprise on him?

If there's one thing that excites a crowd, it is to see a champion performing with power and authority. What excites them even more is to see the champion humbled by a dark horse. The bookmakers like to see it, too.

'Evens on the field,' the small-time bookies murmured. 'Evens on the field bar London.'

They shouldn't have been there. The notices were up at prominent points, *Betting Strictly Prohibited*. Whether on or off duty, members of the local police had mustered in force for their own sports meeting. But in regard to the gambling, they were judicially blind and deaf. It was difficult to stop northcountrymen venturing half a dollar on a runner they fancied. The spirit of the law was observed, people felt, if the little bookies didn't actually stand up on stools and shout the odds to the four winds.

The half-crowns changing hands and the mumbling of mystic formulae passed over my head at the time, though later experience made me understand what had been going on. At similar meetings in the future I even reached such giddy heights of fame that local characters were willing to lay half a dollar on me. And bitterly they complained when I lost them their stake, though they never said anything complimentary when I won. In self-defence I ought to say that I never knew anything of these transactions until after they had taken place. It was trial enough to carry a burden of nervousness in a race without knowing one was also carrying punters' money. However, all this took place in the unregenerate past, before running had become its present merciless, pseudo-scientific business. Who would dream of making a book on a field which included Zatopek or Kuts?

There were many heats in the men's hundred yards, at least a dozen. This being my first sight of adult competition I watched them all with great interest. Now was the chance to learn the secret of real running, to detect that extra ingredient in his make-up which made the true sprinter dominant over other men. Certain technical differences between the competition of men and boys were at once apparent. Many of the men (though not all) wore spiked shoes. Some of them even dug starting holes in the pampered turf of the football pitch. It seemed a popular practice to have cork grips strapped to the hands with elastic rings. I recollected the theory that sprinters competed better if they had some object to grip as they ran. That theory, like so many other notions about athletics, has since been dropped into the bottomless pit of oblivion.

There was certainly a great air of promise about the preparations at the start of the hundred yards track. Men trotted about, flapping their hands, high-stepping with such vigour that they almost struck their chins with their knees.

'Come on, there, Jack!' someone shouted from the crowd.

With a stern, preoccupied mien, Jack waved a hand in response, letting the shouter know that he had the situation well in hand.

'Let's have you, Charlie, lad!' came an encouraging cry from the *aficionado* of a rival sprinter.

Less sober of temperament than Jack, Charlie replied with a smile and a toss of the head and then cavorted away down the side of the track like a startled horse, partly showing off to the girls and partly seeking to put the wind up his opponents by a demonstration of his prowess.

Yes, there was much promise among the seventy or eighty men who jigged about waiting for the blast on the starter's whistle which would screw their nerves up to the last pitch of tautness. Unhappily, the promise did not fruit into fulfilment.

That the heats were exciting could not be denied. It is always exciting to hear the starter's orders ring out over a hushed ground, to see the five or six lightly-clad figures crouch down, to listen for the noise of the gun which will hurl them forward like stones out of a sling, to watch young, fit men striving to best each other in a trial of speed. But most exciting of all is the manner of the striving, if it be well or ill done. Of these men, though not all performed ill, none performed well. All were runners, yet none flashed across the scene like a real runner.

Even the eyes of inexperience could see it. The efforts of these men were little better than the efforts of us schoolboys, scaled up. They seemed to be heavy-footed, making a lot of noise as they moved, remaining too long in contact with the earth in between strides. Bodily attitudes and facial expressions were, many of them, quite extraordinary, especially as the runners neared the winning post. Teeth were clenched in grimaces agonised or ferocious. Heads were thrown back, or wagged from side to side. Arms thrashed out wildly, instead of pumping in planes more or less parallel with the line of motion. Energy was squandered recklessly as torsoes rocked and twisted, after the manner of drowning men striving desperately to grasp a lifeline just out of their reach. Watching, I had the odd impression that some kind of unseen barrier hindered these men. They were clawing at it, battling with it ineffectually, trying in vain to break through it.

12

No such barrier hindered Jack London.

From the moment he came out of his holes I was silent upon a peak in Darien, gazing at the Pacific. This was the revelation. Now I knew the secret. The apprentices had stumbled through the opening scenes, but now the master had arrived to stamp his authority upon the drama. The track became transfigured. Some years still separated me from an acquaintance with Pindar. I didn't even know the brief quotation from the first Olympian which is enshrined in the motto of the Amateur Athletic Association. But the words, if known, would have come to life with Jack London. *Fleetness of foot and flower of strength.* This man had the vital spark. He ran with fire in his belly.

The handicappers had put the big name from the south off scratch. His nearest opponent in the heat had been given five yards, while the front marker was off twelve, almost out of sight of the scratch line. London went after the lot of them as if he hated their guts. So quick were his reactions that he gained at least a yard, and more likely two, on the start. We might have been watching the sudden release of a spring kept under intolerable compression. I had never dreamt that a man could jerk himself into action so instantaneously. Between the start and the build-up to full racing speed one could detect no hesitancy, no awkward changing-up of gear. Smoothly yet ruthlessly the long, lean brown legs developed a stride which cut through the opposition like a sickle cutting through corn stalks. The body was steady, the expression unstrained, the arms and legs driving in parallel planes, the head advancing in a horizontal line that never wavered.

Here were displayed poise and power and purpose. Above all, it was the sense of purpose that imprinted itself upon the mind of the beholder. The man's will vibrated down the track like the twanging of a great bow-string. His racing legs were reaching towards a goal which wasn't a mere line of worsted yarn stretched between two posts, but a claim to supremacy. He flowed along, irresistible, overwhelming, hacking down his opponents' lead as if he were attached to them by a length of rope and were hauling in on it. If you'd never seen running before, you could tell that this athlete was in a different class from his fellow-competitors: and not simply because he was giving them a start and beating them, but because he believed so utterly in what he was doing, his concentration on the task in hand was so complete, his vision of the end so clear. To others, running might be a recreation, or the means of picking up an attractive prize or two. To Jack London, it represented a declaration of himself.

London's victory in the heat was followed by dead silence for an appreciable time. Even the announcement that he had returned evens from scratch did not immediately evoke a cheer. The crowd seemed to need time to come to themselves, as if they were awakening from a dream, before they began to applaud.

'By God,' a man near me said at last, his eyes shining, 'he's got class!'

My own eyes were wide open, as befits one who has seen the light. Naturally, the sight of a champion runner in full cry did not at once transform a young and inexperienced boy into an assured and efficient sprinter. The basic physical ingredients were still lacking. True speed of reaction and strength of muscle only start to come with the quickening of adolescence. But a spark had been touched to the mental fuse. I now had a sense of purpose. In the final of that insignificant little scholars' race for under-twelves I first felt something of the shock of urgency which makes a sprinter. When the gun fired, I went.

CHAPTER TWO

THE MEETING in which Jack London competed was staged under the rules of the Amateur Athletic Association. There are many of these rules, designed in large part to keep athletics pure and unsullied by the taint of professionalism. Perhaps the rule of most concern to the athlete is that he can't compete for a cash prize or for a prize of 'intrinsic value', which means, in effect, a prize that can readily be converted into cash. At the meetings where he competes honour is the only true guerdon, though victory may be sweetened by the gift of a cut-glass vase or an eight-day clock.

In the late nineteen-twenties, the north-east of England was by no means an impregnable stronghold of amateur athletics. Mention the Olympic Games, and it was even money whether the person you spoke to would think of the recent affair held at Amsterdam or the festival of 'pedestrianism' presented under the same lofty title at Morpeth, county town of Northumberland. To the innocent, indeed, the latter might seem to be the more important occasion. Certainly there was a large disparity between the rewards offered to competitors at the two places. At Amsterdam the victor in the 100 metres (P. Williams, of Canada) had the satisfaction of mounting the victory rostrum, seeing his national flag hoisted, and hearing the band play his national anthem, but the tangible payment he received for his labours amounted to no more than a gold medal. At Morpeth, the winner of the 110 yards foot handicap was recompensed with £100, and a proportion of the winnings which his backers collected from their successful bets.

As a young boy, the discrepancy between the newspaper coverage given to these two meetings puzzled me. It was right that such a great international gathering as the Olympic Games at Amsterdam should receive a lot of attention, but it seemed strange that the Morpeth Olympics got no notice at all in the national Press and very little even in our local dailies. I had not yet learnt what a pestilent thing money is when sportsmen compete for it.

Not far from my home was a farm track, where my father often took me to practise running. The track was of ash and clinker, bounded on one side by a thick hawthorn hedge and on the other by a high wall surrounding a lunatic asylum. In May and June the air was sickly sweet with the scent of may blossom, but this had less attraction for a child than the prospect of seeing some poor idiot's face through a first-storey window in one of the asylum blocks. The question whether those within or without the walls were the crazier never occurred.

A boy called Fergus used to join me on these so-called training runs. We were a well-matched pair. A course of eighty or a hundred yards was stepped out for us, and we would run over it several times in an evening. By the time we finished, hot and sweating, neither of us would have shown any marked superiority over the other.

Sometimes other boys came along to swell the number of juvenile athletes to three or four, but after a couple of outings their attendance at the farm track always ceased. They saw no object in this regular toil up and down a cinder lane. I didn't clearly see any object in it myself, for this was before the vision of Jack London and the winning of the twelve and sixpenny suitcase. The running seemed to be labour without reward. My legs got tired, my heart thumped, and often I felt sick. Once or twice I was sick.

Why this peculiar amusement had ever started I didn't know, and even less why it continued. Only so long as Fergus didn't back out of it, I wasn't going to.

Sometimes he and I could hear the shouts of other fellows playing cricket in a nearby field, and the longing to take part in a friendly team game would come over us, a game where you could take your turn at batting or bowling or just lie down in the grass if you felt like it and be forgotten. But we couldn't be forgotten, putting ourselves forward like this as a public spectacle.

Whether he wishes to or not, unless he performs in complete seclusion, the athlete invites the interest of spectators. Our childish exploits on the outskirts of the town attracted a certain amount of notice. This was not by reason of anything notable in the exploits but because the northcountry sportsman cannot resist a contest of any kind, be it between men, boys, horses, dogs or pigeons. Perhaps there was a temporary lull in more adult sporting activity in the neighbourhood. At all events, several local characters got the habit of turning up to witness the duels between Fergus and me. Not only to witness but also to give advice, which was sometimes quite unrealistic.

'You want to run up on your toes, lads,' one character in a flat, checked cap advised. 'Right up on your toes!'

The sprinter certainly thrusts with the ball of the foot and the toes, but he doesn't point on blocked shoes like a ballerina.

'Lean further forward when you're running, lads,' another character urged. His flat cap was black. 'That way the force of gravity helps to give you speed.'

In a stationary position he demonstrated the lean forward, balancing himself by flinging a leg out behind. If we'd taken up such an attitude when actually moving we'd have been helped by the force of gravity in the usual downward direction.

The advice given us, most of it conflicting, tended to pass over our heads. We made little attempt to apply it, though the point did occur to us that grown men thought it worth while offering advice on such a matter as running. Their interest automatically raised the pursuit in our esteem. We got the idea that we were doing something important, if only in a boyish way. When another man in the neighbourhood came along to watch and brought with him a small starting pistol – it didn't make a noise bigger than the crack of a toy whip – we felt that we had been promoted to the senior league. No longer was it necessary for my father to position us, then step off into the distance until he'd paced out the desired course, and finally start us by dropping a handkerchief. Our departure now was much more formal and organised.

It must have been about the time when the man with the pistol appeared that the element of competition began to develop between Fergus and me. Until then Father had been scrupulously fair in the encouragement which he portioned out, not wishing to show partiality towards his son in these friendly contests between two small boys. The result was we ran without feeling that these races were in any way serious competitions. Neither boy made a determined attempt to assert superiority. As yet we were innocent of the fact that life is one long struggle to get the advantage of the other fellow.

That innocence, like other forms of innocence, had to be destroyed.

'Go on, Fergus!' I heard Mr Buglass, the man with the starting pistol, shout one evening. 'Go on, lad! You'll beat him!'

The shouted encouragement gave me a shock that was

almost physical. I had never dreamt that grown-ups could take sides in the matter of these trials between Fergus and me. So far as I knew Mr Buglass wasn't even a relative of my opponent's. And yet, a man of no connection, he could desire Fergus to win. Which meant that he wanted me to lose! The thought made me falter in my stride, like one suddenly beset by enemies. The familiar farm track no longer seemed so friendly. The boy panting away a clear yard ahead of me had ceased to be a pal and had become a rival. This contest wasn't merely fun but an affair of pride and prestige. The sunny summer evening seemed to darken a little. I had a brief, sombre glimpse of the essential solitariness of the athlete, his hand against every man and every man's hand against him. Some of the lightheartedness went out of my attitude, and some determination crept in to replace it.

'Come on, Fergus!'

The shouts were coming from ahead of us now, from the little group of men who stood with my father at the finish. The partisan spirit was definitely abroad. Father sensed that the whole tenor of the relationship between Fergus and me was changing. For the first time he shouted encouragement to me, and I was glad to hear it. It had become very important to win this trial of speed, not because it meant much to me but because it seemed to mean a lot to these men. But Fergus had that clear yard lead over me. In the distance that remained I could chip away some of the yard but I couldn't get it all back. Fergus held off my late challenge. Looking very pleased with himself, sticking his chest out, he lunged over the finishing line roughly scratched across the cinder lane.

His supporters patted him on the back and assured him he was a good little 'un. He turned to me with a challenging look in his eye.

'Well, I beat you,' he said.

Neither of us had ever before boasted of a victory. The pattern of our relationship had indeed changed swiftly.

'My foot slipped,' I said sulkily.

'Go on,' he said. His actual words were 'Gan on', but this isn't the place to attempt to reproduce the *patois* spoken on the banks of the Tyne. 'Your foot didn't slip. I'll beat you again next time we run.'

I glowered. 'No, you won't.'

I was hurt and angry and confused and a little lost. God knows this wasn't much of a challenge that had suddenly loomed up in front of me, but so far life hadn't presented any challenges at all. But I felt that since a challenge had come, it must be responded to.

We stood for a little while, getting our breath back. Mr Buglass came up, gave a congratulatory nod to Fergus, and a pat of consolation to me. I held myself rigid under the pat, scowling. This man was a traitor. He had publicly declared himself against me. It was no use his coming now and trying to smooth things over by assuring my father we were a pair of likely lads. An open enemy was much preferable to a two-faced one. Fergus and I trotted back to the start, followed by Mr Buglass. A couple of sad, vacant faces stared down at us from the windows of the lunatic asylum, faces that only came into view for an instant, and then disappeared.

Already for personal reasons the last race of the evening had become a needle contest, when Mr Gracie arrived to intensify our rivalry with the lure of gold. Mr Gracie was an old man, a retired pit deputy, noble of countenance and patriarchal of bearing. His hair and imperial beard were snow-white. Blue eyes, their keenness only a little dulled by the years, gazed out steadily from under shaggy brows. The facial expression was kindly but firm, the tone of voice authoritative, the carriage erect and dignified. No more respected figure than Mr Gracie lived in the neighbourhood. He came towards us now, plying his walking-stick with a lordly air, the medals chinking on the gold albert stretched across his waistcoat.

'That's the idea, lads,' he commended, as he saw us positioning ourselves on the makeshift starting line. 'There's nothing I like to see more than a race between a pair of boys or young chaps. Youth is the time to develop speed and strength and skill. I used to run myself, you know, when I was a young sprig.'

We looked, too polite to express disbelief that this venerable figure could ever have been a young sprig, or that he could have done anything so frivolous as to hurl himself along a running track.

'Now,' Mr Gracie went on, 'who's going to win this race?'

'I am,' Fergus answered.

'No, he's not,' I said, 'I am.'

The old man chuckled. 'Two proper little fighters, eh? Go to it, lads. Honest, open rivalry helps to make you strong and stops you from being mean. Now, I'll tell you what. Here's sixpence. I'll give it to the winner. That's something to work for, isn't it?'

Our eyes glinted at the prospect of filthy lucre. Sixpence would buy a lot. Such a prize gave extra point to the contest before us. Not only would the winner be able to crow over his defeated rival, but he'd have money in his pocket. As Mr Gracie continued on his way to the finishing line where my father and the other men stood, we looked anxiously at Mr Buglass to see whether he was ready to start us.

Doubtless to the watchers it was no more than a slow, blundering struggle between two kids, neither of them with much idea of running. To us it was life and death. Desperately, agonisingly, we wanted to win. Victory would be a pinnacle of triumph, defeat an abyss of despair. To a small boy a hundred yards seems a very long way, almost a distance race. He doesn't run it in one breath but in many gasps, with much heaving of the chest and much ignorant straining of the muscles, throwing his head back and his arms out as he literally fights with that interminable length of track. Indeed, it much resembles the run-in on the home straight of a hard-fought, closely-contested distance race between men, that last grinding stretch of track where the muscles start to lock with fatigue, and the vision distorts, and the mind reels from cerebral anoxia, and that accursed tape seems to recede instead of advancing.

I'm sure there was never a longer hundred yards race run, nor one fought with grimmer determination, and all for the sake of sixpence and the chance to brag. Whether seriously or jokingly, the onlookers cheered us along, working up an atmosphere of excitement more appropriate to some stern duel between champions. The fact that the lead changed hands between Fergus and me several times fanned the excitement. Until the last few yards it remained in doubt as to who would win. This is what moves a crowd, the delicious agony of doubt, the alternation of hope and fear in a close-run battle. A certainty may be magnificent in his action, but he never engages the sympathy of the onlookers as do well-matched rivals who are striving against each other with all their hearts. A race fought out bitterly the whole way round the last lap will have the crowd in spirit down on the track with the contestants, feeling with them, suffering with them, tasting the sweets of victory and the ashes of defeat. Almost with wonder afterwards the spectators realise that their bodies never left the concrete tiers of the stand. How is it, then, that they are so physically exhausted and drained of energy?

Such are the races that remain in the memory, long after mechanically efficient world record runs have faded into limbo.

So Fergus and I strove with our hearts in an insignificant race between unfledged boys on an obscure farm track in a remote town. Fergus lost. Not by much, but he lost. If you lose by a foot, you may as well have lost by twenty yards. Primacy is everything in racing.

With his slow, dignified gait Mr Gracie walked over to me, said some words of praise, and held out sixpence. My father noticed the action.

'What's that for?' he demanded.

'When I saw the lads down there I promised a prize of sixpence to the winner,' Mr Gracie said. 'It was to give them a bit of encouragement, you know.'

'I don't like it.' The annoyance in my father's tone surprised me. Normally he was mild-mannered. 'The lads run because they want to. Encourage them by all means, but not that way. They shouldn't get any idea of running for money, not even for sixpence.'

'Shouldn't run for money?' Mr Gracie's bushy white eyebrows were raised in astonishment. 'But what's wrong with that? There's got to be some point to a race. If your lad goes up for the Powderhall in a few years' time he'll be running for money, won't he?'

'My boy won't be interested in the Powderhall. He's going to be an amateur.'

'An amateur? Good God!'

Mr Gracie and Mr Buglass and the two men in flat caps stared. Their lives had been hard, and often dangerous. Accustomed to staking existence itself in order to win coal, they could not but see all human activities as a gamble. Sport itself was good, whether racing of horses or men, dogs or birds: whether pitching of quoits in a clay-pit: whether

23

the fist-fighting of two young sparks over a girl: whethe
bowling for length with a tar ball over the flat, smooth
stretches of sand revealed at low water. But what gave tha
final zest to sport was the venturing of a few bob on you
fancy, or the hope of gaining a money prize.

The sixpence was still clutched in my hand. On a signa
from my father I offered it back, with some reluctance, t
Mr Gracie. The old man shook his head irritably.

'No, no, keep it. Share it with the other lad here.' H
turned to my father. 'Unless you think that's going to mak
them forfeit their amateur status?'

All idylls have their end, and this one now drew toward
its close. Fergus began to show less interest in running
Having lost the first race which was of any importance t
us, the first race in which something was at stake, h
allowed me to get the mental edge over him. A boy is easil
disheartened. If, after some experience of football, he find
that he never scores a goal, he may well decide that this i
a pointless game. Or his appetite for cricket will flag if h
discovers that he isn't thought good enough to bat or bow
and must spend most of his time fielding at long stop. A
young boy who isn't a good player by nature will rarely si
down and work out how he can make himself a good
player by artifice. After the affair of the sixpence Fergu
and I had only a few races. He lost every one. It wa
obvious that he would soon retire from a contest that h
now regarded as unequal. The two men in flat caps, on
checked and the other black, brought our relationship t
an end abruptly.

We had toiled once again over the cinder path betweer
the hawthorn hedge and the high wall. Until well past th
half-way mark Fergus kept level with me. He might hav
won had not the prospect of victory excited him so tha
he over-reached himself and stumbled. By the time h

recovered I was too far ahead to be overtaken.

Checked cap and black cap seemed to show an unusual interest in the result of the race. As I crossed the line there came a chink of money. Checked cap, who was red-cheeked and beefy, held out his hand. Black cap, tallow-faced, sad, and slightly stooped, put something into it. The beefy character signalled me over. He had a broad smile on his face.

'Here you are, son,' he said, holding out a coin. 'You did the work. Why shouldn't you take a cut of the winnings? Buy yourself a few sweets.'

Not knowing what went on, but recollecting the lecture I'd got after the affair of Mr Gracie's sixpence, I kept my hands behind my back.

'No, thanks,' I stammered, 'my father said I wasn't to take money prizes.'

'But this isn't a prize.'

'N-no, thanks.'

'Howway, lad, take it.'

'What's going on here?' My father had suddenly come up behind us.

'It's nowt.' Checked cap looked embarrassed. 'Nowt to speak of. Me and Geordie here had half a dollar on that bit race. I backed your lad to win, so I just thought I'd give him a few coppers for himself.'

Breathing deeply, Father knocked away the hand holding the money. 'You ought to be damn well ashamed of yourself,' he said, 'betting on a couple of kids running.'

'Why, what's the matter with that? Before now I've bet on a couple of frogs, which could jump the farthest.'

'Frogs aren't like boys. They haven't got heads you can put ideas into. Give your mate his money back.'

'Give him his——?' Checked cap was open-mouthed with surprise and indignation. 'But I won it fair and square.

A level half-dollar, that's what we laid each other.'

'And I say you had no right to lay anything!' Father shouted. 'If these lads want to take part in sport it's going to be clean sport, so long as I have any say in the matter. Bring money into it, and it won't be clean. It'll be damned dirty. Next thing is you'll be wanting them to run to bookie's orders, or turn out under false names, or put lead soles in their shoes. That's the sort of tricks they play at Morpeth, and at the Powderhall. I don't even want my boy to hear about such a rotten game, let alone take part in it. So give your mate his money back!'

'Steady on, Jack,' checked cap blustered. My father's name was Billy. 'Jack' was a local form of address. 'Chap can do what he likes with his own.'

'Give the money back!' Father said in a passion.

Sulkily checked cap returned to his pocket whatever donation he'd intended for me, took out half a crown, and flipped it over to black cap.

'Bet's off, Geordie,' he said.

To avoid the possibility of further contamination from the betting fraternity, races on the farm track ceased to be held.

My father's strictures on 'pedestrianism' were, I think, over-harsh. There have been plenty of decent, sporting professional runners, men who ran because they liked running, men who would have shown up well in whatever sphere of athletics they had chosen to compete. No one could have doubted the ability or the integrity of the Glasgow runner, W. McFarlane, winner of the Powderhall Handicap in 1933 and 1934, the second time, almost unbelievably, from scratch.

Yet that there should be some dirt in the professional game is inevitable. At the Powderhall or the Morpeth

26

Olympics money is at stake. And not the prize money only, nor even first in importance, but the cash gambled by the punters on their fancied runners. This isn't a matter of an odd half-crown staked illicitly at an amateur meeting in a colliery district. The bookies are out in force with satchels full of pound notes. And where the punters are gathered, and the bookies, and the easy money, there also congregate the touts and sharks and strong-arm boys. The atmosphere of the running is entirely wrong. Spectators cheer on their man not because they're excited by this contest of strength and speed that he's engaged in but because they've managed to get long odds on him and hope to clear a packet. The runners themselves are bound to be affected by such an atmosphere. Often they are advised that it would pay their backers if they dropped a race rather than if they won it. Out of any gains so acquired the runner will get his cut. So the opportunities for fraud and deceit and poor sportsmanship increase and multiply.

No, the amateur way is the better way, and also, which happens in few other sports now, the more efficient, the more productive of high standards. Yet, looked at object-ively, amateur running may well seem a daft pursuit. In it grown men challenge each other as to who can run the fastest over a quite arbitrarily chosen distance. In deciding that challenge they will probably run themselves into a state of acute discomfort, if not of actual exhaustion. And there is no tangible object of their chase. A greyhound has the incentive of an electric hare to pursue, in default of a live one, or the scent of an aniseed bag trailed along the ground. Man, superior to the animals by virtue of his reason, chases nothing more substantial than a line of worsted yarn stretched between two posts. Later, as a reward for snapping the worsted first, he may be given a certificate to show that he did snap the worsted first. Or possibly he will receive a pair of electro-plated salad servers, to add to the store of electro-plated salad servers which he has already amassed through other victories. Such acknowledgment of his efforts seems inadequate. It certainly does not reimburse him for the quite considerable sum of money which he may have spent on entrance fee and travelling expenses.

There would undoubtedly be more sense in athletics if the runner's objective, instead of the tape, were the prize table, and if that prize table were heaped with gold coin and precious jewels to be seized on the 'first come, first served' principle. That was how foot racing began, though somehow the idea got lost at quite an early stage in the history of this peculiar exercise.

To be precise, the first foot race offered as prize a desirable female, the principal competitor herself, Atalanta. (One does not quite know how the A.A.A. would have regarded such a prize, unless a female could be classified as 'an object of intrinsic value', readily convertible into cash.) Atalanta was a considerable performer in different fields of sport. Having taken part with Meleager in the hunting of the great Calydonian boar, she decided that marriage was not a suitable career for a woman of her ability in the chase. When, in defiance of her publicly-professed distaste for the thought of matrimony, suitors arrived at her father's court to seek her hand, she devised a way of ridding herself of their importunities. A herald proclaimed that the only suitor Atalanta would marry would be one who could beat her in a foot race (distance unspecified). Those who tried themselves against her and failed should pay forfeit with their lives.

The choice at once cooled the ardour of many suitors. Atalanta was well known as a very fast mover on the track. Some who tried their luck lost not only the race but also their heads, which were stuck up on poles around the course. The sight had a lowering effect on later wooers, until Hippomenes came along with the three golden apples given to him by Aphrodite and tricked Atalanta into defeat by throwing one of the baubles in front of her whenever she threatened to gain a commanding lead. Atalanta was willing to concede the race, and herself, for the sake of the gold.

Gold in the days of legend, mink and diamonds in the modern era. Woman, it seems, does not change much.

That early race was merely a single event, held in rather unusual circumstances. Our first record of an organised sports meeting, the kind of meeting which can be regarded as the true precursor of modern athletics occasions, occurs in book XXIII of the *Iliad*, where Achilles promotes games as part of the funeral ceremonies held in honour of his recently-killed friend Patroclus. Several events were included in the programme, among them a foot race. As prizes for this the promoter, from whom the ultra-amateur Achilles Club later took its name, offered a great silver bowl, a mighty ox, and half a talent of gold. Under A.A.A. rules the three warriors who took those prizes would clearly have forfeited their amateur status. But the Homeric heroes had a business instinct. They settled for cash, or sometimes for a pretty slave girl. Their rough, untutored epoch must have been the high noon of professional running. The amateur game developed later. It wasn't from Mycenae but from Sparta that we got this odd notion of running races for the sake of honour and glory, with a wreath of wild olive thrown in.

CHAPTER THREE

ALTHOUGH MY FULL ENTRY into the society of athletes did not take place for several years after the vision of Jack London, it seems to me that from the start I had a vague inkling of what a restricted and strangely private society it is. Not an exclusive society. Far from it. Anyone may be admitted to membership. But the mere fact of his wishing to be a member will mean that he has already marked himself off from his fellow-men.

The distinction between the runner and the non-runner arises not from any specialist technique or mysteries of the craft so much as from the ethos of athletics. The athlete does not embark upon a sport but upon a way of life. That way of life is solitary and self-oriented. When he joins a club a novice runner may think that he has attached himself to a social group, whereas in fact he has declared himself unsocial, he has opted for loneliness. During his long periods of training and preparation that will become apparent to him, but the full measure of his solitude will only strike him in the moment of truth, when he gets down to his blocks or comes up to the starting line. A modern St Simon Stylites, seeking to mortify himself through physical discomfort and separation from his fellows, would be well advised to buy a pair of spiked shoes instead of finding a pillar to sit on.

'Why should you want to climb a mountain?' they used to ask Whymper.

'Because it's there,' he replied.

It's difficult to think of any more reasonable answer to

give when people ask why you chose to be an athlete. The fact that the question can be put is in itself significant. It means that you are doing something the rest of the world does not find it easy to comprehend. Competition the non-athlete can understand, even if it be competition offering the winner no great reward in material goods or renown. Girls compete in beauty contests, children at the seaside in the building of sandcastles, gardeners in the production of marrows. It isn't so much out of the way, then, for men to make trial against each other of their speed or strength. But what the non-athlete doesn't understand so easily is that the athlete should submit himself for many years to the rigorous routine of training. What the non-athlete doesn't understand at all is that the athlete should continue to suffer such a routine even though it may lead him to few or no successes in competition, or when he has no intention of ever putting himself forward for competition.

Returning from a club run through winter streets and country lanes we would hear the comments of men standing at street corners. As a sprinter I hated such runs, which required me to cover a distance of five or six miles instead of a measured furlong. Always I brought up the rear, by a sizeable margin. Feet and legs would be splashed with mud, toes blistered, vest soaking with sweat, mouth parched and sticky with dried spit, lungs heaving and sobbing, and quite likely there would be a painful, stabbing stitch in the side as well. At that moment my greatest desire in the world would be to stop running. Nothing prevented me realising that desire except sheer obstinacy. Instead of stopping, I would urge my aching legs into a travesty of a finishing sprint.

The local club had its winter headquarters in a public house. Always, on training nights, there seemed to be a group of men who forsook the pleasures of the bar for the interest of watching the runners come in.

'God Almighty, here's another of them,' a man would comment. 'Must be the loonies' night out.'

'Proper barmy,' one of his mates would agree.

'Right up the pole. Go on, lad, catch your pals up. They only got here half an hour ago.'

'You'd think a chap would have more sense. What does he want to do a thing like this for?'

The speaker wasn't the only one asking that question, and not getting a very satisfactory answer to it. Feet thudding on the pavement as I covered the last few yards I would wonder yet again at my folly, and resolve that this was the last time I would tolerate such pointless labour, with all the aches and pains that it entailed. But it never was the last time. The labour had a fascination. Some part of my nature seemed to find self-expression through performing it. Yet why the runner's nature should require such expression while the non-runner's didn't was a mystery hard to penetrate.

Perhaps, in a queer way, the runner is seeking communion with Nature. I don't suggest he performs a ritual half-mile in the same way that other and more exotic characters perform a ritual fire dance (although in heroic times athletic sports were part of the funeral rites with which deceased warriors were urged on their way to the next world) but there is a feeling, which comes more in solitary training than in the stress of competition, that you are in harmony with something greater than yourself. Some might describe this feeling as no more than Joy through Strength, and satisfaction is certainly to be derived from knowing that the body is perfectly tuned for the function of moving at speed over short distances or with endurance over long. But what end lies beyond the function? Why does the mere act of running, divorced from all thought of

32

contest, bring contentment? Is the runner groping towards something which other men don't see? Work, sacrifice, dedication, these concepts have a familiar ring about them, and not only in the field of sport.

As far as he can the athlete gives expression to his 'virtue', using the word in its original sense of *vir-tus*, or manliness, the quality of being a *vir*. The particular excellences of a man are courage, strength, endurance, purpose, and it is the assertion of these qualities in a contest far beyond the normal limits of physical effort that marks the true athlete. Where the spirit is willing, the weakness of the flesh is merely a handicap to overcome, not a barrier to halt at.

If the non-runner regards the runner with wondering derision, often enough the runner regards the non-runner with pitying contempt: the contempt of a man who has a belief for the man who hasn't, the contempt of a man driven by a sense of purpose for the man who isn't, the contempt of the man who knows that the body must be made subservient to the dictates of the will for the man whose will seems to have no power of dictation at all.

Think of the young runner as a fool, and you must think of the older runner as a bigger fool. The grey hairs of a grandfather do consort a little oddly with spiked shoes and a track suit, yet there are many men into the fabric of whose lives running has been so inextricably woven that they shrink from cutting it out almost as much as they would shrink from the amputation of a limb. J. T. Holden, of Tipton Harriers, first won the International Cross-country Championship in 1933. During the same season he gained his first national track title, winning the A.A.A. Six Miles. Eighteen years including a world war later, Holden was still a competitor of international class, although by then he had abandoned the track for the longer distances on the road, especially the Marathon. The man's hair had

33

grizzled and his face showed the lines of experience and authority, but his middling-sized, deep-chested, muscular figure was as youthful as ever. More than that, the knife-edge of his mind, far from being blunted by so many years of bitter competition, so many thousands of miles ground out over road and country in all weathers, was still keen. People speak of the killer instinct of Zatopek and Kuts, of their ability to win a race from in front by cracking their opponents through ruthless pace setting, as if this were some new phenomenon. Holden had been an aggressive, hard-driving runner before Zatopek was ever heard of. Nearly at the end of his career, when he went up for the start of the European Games Marathon in 1950, he drew the attention of Continental competitors to the Union Jack on the front of his vest.

'Take a good look at this now,' he told them, 'because it's the last chance you'll have of seeing it before the finish.' And it was so.

Having in his time broken many other runners, Holden himself was at last broken by J. H. Peters in the Polytechnic Marathon of 1951.

If a man pursues one particular activity for long enough, even if it be an activity as incomprehensible to the general public as pushing a pea with his nose, he eventually makes himself an institution. In athletics, Jack Holden was a national institution. Paddy Blane was also an institution, but on the smaller scale of our north-east coast town and its surrounding district.

No one knew exactly how old Paddy was. He seemed coyly uncertain on the point himself. At least fifty, and probably rather more. Fifty is no great age, though a generation ago it was considered a good deal more advanced than it is now, yet it's certainly quite an age for a runner in active competition. But Paddy had got beyond

34

the point where people expressed surprise at seeing such an old-timer still hoofing it through the streets. They were proud of him, counting him a card, a character, a colourful feature of the local scene.

'There's old Paddy,' they said, as they huddled under umbrellas in driving rain at a tram stop and watched the short figure splashing past them through the puddles.

Or when the snowflakes swirled down thickly, drawing a candid curtain over the buildings and muffling the sound of padding feet on the roads, women would sometimes start back in alarm as a figure loomed out of the white storm, panting breath billowing in clouds, bald pate covered by a handkerchief knotted at the four corners, snow crusting itself on the sodden vest but melting on the heated, sweat-stained face.

'Oh, it's only old Paddy,' the women would say, exhaling with relief that it wasn't Jack the Ripper, and having an odd comforting belief that the blizzard-swept night could now hold no terrors. For the appearance of Paddy's familiar figure must mean that all was normal. 'Don't get stuck in a drift now, Paddy,' they would giggle.

Rarely did Paddy hear the witticisms passed as he trudged through the dirty, dark, dismal streets. When a man is tired and intent on nothing except to finish a gruelling course, you can fire a 4-inch gun in his ear and he will be no more than vaguely aware of a detonation. But if he did hear, he grinned his toothless grin and waved a hand in friendly acknowledgment. What he never did was to stop running. Endlessly the short, bandy-legged figure gyrated through the winter streets of our town, or toiled over the country roads leading to Sunderland or Newcastle. Going from his lodgings to his job as storekeeper in an engineering works, Paddy ran. Returning in the evening, he ran. Some spring inside the man had been wound up, and never seemed to wind down. So far as anyone knew, he was unmarried. Certainly he had no wife or close relatives in the district. Except within the brotherhood of athletes he formed no friendships, nor did he develop any interests. He did his five and a half day stint in the engineering works, he ate, presumably he slept, and he spent the rest of his time running. Running was his life. Every weekday he ran. On Sundays he walked.

Those who believe that the typical athlete should be physically developed like the Hermes of Praxiteles would never have put Paddy Blane down as a runner, not with his bandy legs and short stature and long arms and bald head and almost toothless gums. Indeed, with his peculiar frame he would probably not have been a successful man on the track, for the track is a less natural arena of competition than the road and seems to exact from its adherents certain standards of bodily proportion.

On the quarter-mile oval nature complies with the prescriptions of art. In order to give a good performance, a machine must be well designed and engineered. The same holds good of the human body. Thus, as a rule the sprinter will be a little above medium height, with a well-developed torso and strongly-muscled, but not thick or heavy, legs. He must be so constructed that he can operate entirely on strength in hand, not needing to replenish that strength, as it is dissipated, with an intake of oxygen. The distance man is leaner than the sprinter and often a little taller. His build permits him to mount a prolonged effort over many minutes, or even several hours, during which controlled breathing prevents a rapid breakdown of his tissues and recruits energy to replace energy expended through work. The sprinter can run a long distance, but slowly and without enjoyment due to his poor oxygen conversion rate. Except in the form of a 'drive', the distance man cannot sprint, since his muscular reactions are never quick enough for a rapid recovery of stride. No matter how much he practises, neither man will ever overcome this basic defect in his make-up.

At least, he cannot overcome it to the extent of gaining distinction in the higher echelons of an event opposed in the scale to his own. Some decathlon performers do well over all track distances up to 1,500 metres, but judged by world standards their performances cannot rank as better than average. E. Zatopek could not possibly have been a sprinter, while J. C. Owens never tried any distance above a furlong.

Apart from such broad distinctions, there is no *beau idéal* of the athlete, no type to whom you can point, not knowing him, and say, 'He must be a runner.' In his street clothes, or in the working rig appropriate to factory or shipyard, the athlete may not cut a striking figure, especially if observed at rest. But observe him in motion when he has stripped and gone out on to track or road. Then you can recognise him for what he is by the ease and economy and rhythm of his movements, by the poise of his body, by the assurance of his manner. Let a good oarsman step into a racing shell and he and the craft become one entity. The two are quite at home with each other. A similar impression can be got from watching a trained and experienced runner at work on a track. The man belongs there. He is the reason of the track's being, and the track the reason of his. The association of the two seems as natural as the association of a knife and fork.

Runners, then, are a mixed lot. Except for the dwarf and the giant, the emaciated and the obese, they come in most shapes and sizes. Only one thing do they all share and that is determination, a degree of determination often great enough to overcome physical handicaps which the normal person would regard as incapacitating.

A man whose name I have long forgotten lost an arm in an accident. He was a middle distance runner, a frequent competitor at local meetings in Northumberland and Durham. Though the name be forgotten, the image of the man himself is quite clear in the memory, and his fair hair, and his green-and-white hooped vest, and his white shorts. Clear also is the vision of that flabby stump – the arm having been amputated not far short of the shoulder – protruding through the half-sleeve of the vest. No doubt, as someone said with rather rough humour, it would have been a much greater handicap to his running if he had lost a leg, but a missing arm troubles a man far more than might be thought. Several pounds in weight are missing from one side of his body. He is unbalanced, and must adjust his posture. Counter-balancing by a lean towards the armless side is the obvious compensation to make, but it doesn't noticeably help forward progress. With only one upper limb it is difficult to mount an arm-drive, that pumping movement which forces more air into failing lungs and thus transmits a last flicker of energy to heavy and aching legs. Finally, the tactical disadvantage at which the lost limb put the runner was not slight. With only one arm he could not help himself much in that mad rush to the first bend in a half-mile, when fists flail and bodies jostle and a sharp elbow in the ribs is a man's reward for hindering the advance of an opponent anxious to get to the front. Yet the one-armed runner surmounted these handicaps. He asked for no quarter in the hurly-burly of middle-distance racing, and I don't think he got much. How often he finished in the first three was a question, but he was always in there, trying.

George Elliott also suffered a disability, not so disfiguring and yet more serious. In the days of the Ottoman Empire the *bastinado* was applied to the soles of the feet of a peccant cavalryman so that he could at least still sit a horse afterwards. It was applied to the posterior of an infantryman, so that he could at least still march. The athlete is in much the same position as the Turkish infantryman. So long as his legs and feet remain whole and uninjured, he is not debarred from his sport. George Elliott's feet did not remain whole.

A heavy casting slipped from a badly secured sling in the dockyard fitting shop where Elliott worked. He was lucky. A straight fall of the casting would have sliced off his right foot without benefit of surgery. But the block of metal swung before it fell and only caught Elliott a glancing blow as he got out from under. The glancing blow from half a ton of steel fractured and splintered every metatarsal bone. When they took an X-ray photograph of the foot at the local Infirmary the radiographer said that setting this job would be more a problem for a jigsaw puzzle expert than a surgeon.

The bones were set and put in plaster, and when the plaster came off it turned out that the foot was crooked, so the bones had to be broken again under anaesthetic and re-set. It was a long process and Elliott did not suffer it patiently, for he was an active man and a keen harrier.

'Come on, doc,' he urged, 'get a bloody move on. The season'll be over before we can get back on the roads again.'

Not taking him seriously, the doctor laughed. He considered it would be quite an achievement on his part if he got his patient to the point of walking again with reasonable efficiency. Something in the laugh caught Elliott's attention. He looked at the other man for a long moment.

'We're going to be all right, aren't we, doc? You're fettling this foot for us?'

39

'Perfectly all right,' the doctor soothed. 'There's nothing to worry about. By the time we finish with you in here and perhaps give you some electro-therapy in Out-patients you should be able to get about quite normally.'

The doctor didn't realise that, to Elliott, an essential part of normalcy was the ability to run. A foot was a useless object unless it would stand up to the strain of a ten-mile pounding on tarmacadam roads. Even before his discharge from the out-patients' department George Elliott began to submit his foot to that test. When it didn't pass satisfactorily, he complained to the doctor.

'Good God.' The doctor looked shocked. 'You don't mean to tell me you're actually running on that foot?'

'Why, aye.'

'But that's crazy. The bones are weak.'

'You said the foot'd be all right again.'

'Of course, but I meant all right for ordinary purposes. It can never be as strong as it was before the fracture. If you submit the bones to any undue strain they'll almost certainly give way under it. Unless you stop running, my friend, you take the risk of crippling yourself!'

Elliott shook his head obstinately. 'If I stopped running I'd be no better than a bloody cripple, anyway, so I may as well carry on and make a right job of it.'

'Well, it's your foot.'

I met Elliott some time later, coming back to the club headquarters one evening. It was bitter weather, with a cruel north-east wind blowing that cut a man to the bone. Those people who had ventured abroad were hunched down into their overcoats, looking frozen. Yet George, wearing only a vest and shorts, was sweating. Agony, not heat, induced the perspiration. Deep lines of pain were carved down his face from nose to lower jaw-line. A faint tremor shook his right leg. Every time he put that foot down on the road, he winced. Yet, when he saw me, he smiled.

'How are things going, George?'

'Not so bad, you know. Not so bad.' He took in a deep breath. 'I've just run a mile. It's the longest distance I've managed since my accident. Maybe by next week I'll jack it up to two miles.'

'But doesn't the foot hurt?'

'Oh, aye, the foot's jibbing a bit. But if a chap stopped running every time he got a bit ache or pain, then he'd never run at all, would he?'

There have been many cases besides George Elliott's of runners who refused to give in to physical infirmities. They regarded the body as a recalcitrant beast which had to be mastered. Even when it is whole and sound, the runner still finds his body recalcitrant. It accepts and even likes a moderate amount of exercise, but it does not like a lot. Once the golden mean is passed, it has to be driven. In running, one always seems to be faced with these questions of compulsion. Why should a man be urged to run in the first place? Why should he urge his body to take part in an activity which it only too often finds distasteful? Why should he keep on urging it long after the point when any reasonable person would consider the object of the exercise to have been achieved? Having run a half-mile in one minute fifty seconds, why should he want to run it in one minute forty-nine? Is there any limit to the amount of compulsion which the body will accept? Or to the speed at which it can be driven?

Presumably there is, but we do not know it. Of the two extremes of bodily capacity we can be certain only of one, which is zero. The other is x, an unknown quantity. Sometimes we seem to be reaching a point where we can determine the value of x, as when four minutes was thought to be the best possible time for the mile, but then along comes someone like R. G. Bannister to make hay of hardening opinion and to leave the definition of x as far off as ever.

It is in the middle and longer distances that we are vaguest about the possible upper limit of physical effort, for times over these distances have shortened regularly ever since formal competition in them was started in the modern era. In the hundred yards, by contrast, maximum effort was registered quite early on, or so it would seem from the little improvement that has taken place over the years. The A.A.A. championship event was first won in 'level time' in 1886, and 'level time' was also recorded by the winner in 1957. Ten seconds, in fact, is still a respectable time for the short sprint, even in the United States where the best men normally cover the distance in about nine and a half seconds. So in this event at least we should be able to give an approximate value for x.

Yet can we?

The hundred yards dash is about as far as a man can run without drawing breath. The speed and manner of his movement do not allow him to establish any regular cycle of air intake. Most runners therefore draw a few deep breaths before the start and then rely on the oxygen reserve thus built up. Some runners, however, manage to draw a breath at about the sixty or seventy yards mark in the race, though it is something they must do automatically and without conscious planning, otherwise they will break their concentration and this in turn will break the rhythm of their movement.

There is no doubt that a breath so taken gives a sudden, galvanising surge of speed. Only once can I plainly remember it happening to me, in a match between Cambridge-shire A.A.A. and the C.U.A.C. on Jesus Green in Cambridge. In the early stages of the hundred yards I ran poorly. Perhaps not enough deep breathing had been done before the start. At all events, by the sixty yards mark I found myself two yards astern of the second last runner, and likely to remain so. At that point it was possibly a gasp of horror that I gave rather than a deliberate breath that I took, but the effect was blinding. The other competitors still moved but not, seemingly, at more than a gentle canter, whereas my own speed had become a gallop. There was that glorious sensation which is felt when your opponents come back to you without effort on your part, as if all at once your performance had been raised to a quite different category from theirs. Within twenty yards I had passed two of the runners and pulled up level with the leader. Within another twenty I was two yards ahead of him. There had been no effort, no strain, no grunting earth-bound toiling. This was aerial rather than terrestrial movement. Those last forty yards, in which nearly five were gained, must have been covered at a rate much higher than my average even for a respectable run. What sort of time would be returned if one could establish that higher rate over the full hundred yards? And if it can't be established, why not?

When the human constitution is called on to make a severe physical effort various factors, such as the build-up of fatigue products, act on it as brakes. Intensive training, and will-power, can defer the moment when the brakes are applied. But quite apart from the brakes some kind of interior governor seems to be at work inhibiting and regulating our effort even when the will demands that the effort should be made with the throttle fully open. Every runner knows the feeling that he could run faster if only something inside would let him, something which is more than the apparently limiting factor of muscular strength. Unhappily we cannot identify that restraint and are therefore

43   D

unable to assess the chances of its being lifted. But we do know that in certain unnatural conditions the governor ceases to operate. In the extremes of rage or pain or fear all brakes and restraints, of whatever nature, come off. Men perform physical feats quite outside the normal range of their capacity. I saw a striking instance of this, once.

At about the time when I first became interested in running, real running, we had a neighbour called Octavus Wilson. Although he was a dockmaster on the river, a job which one would have thought called for lung power and assertiveness, 'Tavus had a soft voice and a mild manner. He and his wife were childless, and led a quiet, secluded existence. What strains in his private life or in his occupation were the cause, no one seemed to know, but 'Tavus went mad. He went mad in no very violent way, but nevertheless he went mad. The word had a stigma attached to it. They were going to come and take him away. Mrs Wilson was distraught. Gossip spread through the neighbourhood. Many people were sorry, some were not so sorry, and some took a mournful pleasure in contemplating the witless condition of a fellow-mortal. Although the doctors said visits were permissible and might be beneficial to the patient, there was a reluctance to cross the Wilsons' threshold. Nobody wanted to face a madman. Nobody knew how such a confrontation might turn out.

My father went. Without his realising it, as he was talking to Mrs Wilson, I slipped in behind and followed up the stairs. Curiosity moved me mainly, but also some desire to tell 'Tavus that I felt sorry for him. Perhaps because he had none of his own he was always kind to children, rarely passing without the gift of a copper or a few sweets. The grownups had got to the bedroom door and opened it before they saw I was there. They let me stay, possibly because they

44

thought the disturbance of shooing me away would upset the sick man, possibly because they were too preoccupied with their thoughts to pay me proper attention.

It was evidently not the connubial chamber which we entered. A single bed stood in a small room which had little space to hold more than that and a washhand-stand. The bed had metal railed ends, topped with polished brass knobs. 'Tavus was sitting up in it, propped against pillows, clad in striped flannel pyjamas. I stared at him eagerly, looking for signs of madness, thinking to see some horrifying change in his face. But at first glance the round red features seemed the same as usual.

'Hullo, there, 'Tavus,' my father said heartily.

'Why, hullo, Billy.'

'I just dropped in to see how you were getting on.'

'Why, now, that's very neighbourly. Come on in, man. Sit down, sit down. Just pull up that chair over there.'

There was no chair to be pulled up. That struck me as odd. Another odd thing was 'Tavus's conversation. Once he'd started he went on, almost without pause. Normally he had little to say to people, but now his tongue was unloosed. Words poured out. The words made sense, but they were trivial. I regarded 'Tavus's face more closely. There was a change in it, but too subtle a change to define accurately. Was I now seeing it through a curtain which hadn't been there before, or was I seeing it unscreened by a curtain which had been there before?

'So you're feeling all right?' my father asked.

'I'm feeling grand, Billy. Couldn't be better. But, you know, they're saying I've got to go away. I've told them I don't want to go, but they're saying I have to.'

Father coughed. 'Well, of course, 'Tavus, you're not absolutely well. The doctor just thinks a spell in hospital might do you good.'

45

'But I don't want to go to hospital.' The blue eyes were staring now in the round, red face. 'There's no need for me to go. It's only Minnie here, trying to push me out of the way.'

'No, no, you mustn't say that. She simply wants to do what's best for you.'

'That's what they all say. They all say they know best. They all want me out of the way.' The voice was rising. 'I don't need to go to hospital. Why can't I stay at home? I've never felt better in my life.'

'Now, 'Tavus, you have to let the doctor decide that.'

'I've never felt better in my life. I'm full of strength. Did you know how strong I've got since they put me in bed?'

'You were always quite a powerful man, 'Tavus.'

'Oh, but I'm really strong now,' 'Tavus giggled. 'Just you watch.'

The two pallid arms, in their casing of striped flannel, reached out. One grasped the rail at the head of the bed, the other the rail at the foot. Although it was a short bed, the arms were fully extended. Then they pulled. I couldn't believe anything would happen. That was iron the man had hold of. You couldn't bend iron, not just like that. But 'Tavus did. And he wasn't in a rage, nor straining unduly. With a silly smile on his face he heaved, and the rails began to curve under his grip. The castors squealed on the floor as the legs leaned outwards in sympathy with the inward slant of the rails. We were witnessing the exertion of untrammelled power, power hedged about by no inhibitions, the power of a man who was using himself utterly, to the last ounce, a man who had no doubts. Never, in his sanity, could 'Tavus Wilson have attempted such a feat. Now, in his madness, it came to him easily.

My father went white. 'My God,' he whispered, as he took a step which interposed himself between me and the

46

man in the bed. Then I was pushed out of the room by Mrs Wilson and the door shut behind me.

Unnatural strength filled 'Tavus Wilson because he was off his head. Possessed by agony when they first took the dressings from the shattered stumps of his legs, Douglas Bader performed a similar bed-bending feat. Yet the strength must have been in these men all the time. There was no pouring in of power from outside. Pain or dementia simply released something that was already present, allowed its full deployment without the inhibition of any governor. It would seem that we have two reservoirs of energy inside us, the one which we tap when in normal possession of our faculties, and the other, a dark, mysterious reservoir, which becomes available to us when we are beside ourselves.

Such a thought fascinates the runner when he is speculating about the final physical effort of which the human frame is capable. All about him he sees the peaks of endeavour which have so far been scaled, peaks which, year by year, have grown a little higher. But beyond those peaks there must be supreme heights which are also scaleable if only the athlete could win the knowledge to release the barrier damming up that last, mysterious reservoir of energy.

Or is it the case that, to a man in his senses, such a release can never come? Perhaps because that last reservoir constitutes sanity itself?

CHAPTER FOUR

ALL RUNNERS ARE LONELY. Some are more lonely than others.

For the members of a big and active University athletics club the essential solitariness of their pursuit may be concealed, or at least compensated for, by the companionship of the other men in the club, by the horseplay in the pavilion, by the shared motor-car and train journeys, by residence in the same hotel or private house when on tour.

Yet the knowledge of each other which athletes may get from such association is never as profound as when footballers or cricketers come together. For a cricketer's acquaintance with and understanding of his team-mates is based on an interest shared with them and on the necessity of working with them towards a common end. Athletes in a team may appear to share the same goal, but in reality they do not. Their hands are against every man. In the hundred yards the second string will be fired by a suitable urge to beat the sprinters of the opposing team. But he will also be moved by a desire to beat his own first string. His aim is self-oriented, the aim of a man who walks alone, even though this may lie concealed under surface bonhomie.

Nevertheless the companionship of a big club, and the facilities it has to offer, help to sweeten the pill of loneliness and single-handed endeavour. But a generation ago, and especially in parts of the country north of the Humber, there were none of the facilities and often little of the companionship which might help to cheer a runner in his solitary toil.

Nowadays, probably, a tide of council houses has closed in on either side of the railway which I have in mind, but in those days the metal tracks drew a dead straight line for almost three miles across coarse and marshy pastureland. A low embankment, built up from ash and clinker, supported the tracks. On one side, between the edge of the embankment and the ballast cradling the sleepers, ran a path about two yards wide. Railwaymen used a section of the path as a short cut to get to their work in the Simonside loco sheds and marshalling yard. Grave, responsible-looking characters, they walked over the cinders swinging their bait boxes and tea cans, identifiable for what they were by the blue dungaree jacket and trousers and the mackintosh peaked cap which comprised the uniform of their trade. In such company another regular user of the path seemed out of place. He also wore a uniform, but it symbolised a vocation rather than a trade. It consisted of a cotton vest, black satin shorts, and spiked shoes. While the railway workers moved over the grey ash surface at a stolid plod, the runner drove himself along in violent, body-racking bursts of speed. Sprinters needed a cinder track, it was said, if they were to perform at their best. This was the only cinder track available to the runner.

To the south of the railway embankment a rural village lay on gently rising ground. To the north, approaching the banks of the Tyne, the apparatus of industry had inflicted many mutilations on a sombre landscape. On the one side could be heard the song of a hovering lark, on the other the distant, metallic chatter of pneumatic riveters. But the runner had no eyes for the contrast between farmyards and slag-heaps, meadows and pitheads, church spires and giant cranes. He had no ears for the puff of shunting engines in the marshalling yard, the buffers clanging like a recurring decimal, the screech of metal wheel upon metal rail. His vision was turned inwards, upon himself, and not upon the external scene.

Sometimes with a rush and slam of air the Newcastle to Middlesbrough express flung past him, its power and speed making a mock of his little endeavours. Local trains, approaching or leaving the little country station nearby, proceeded more slowly, so that in a flat-out sprint the runner could keep pace with the grimy coaches, or even overtake them. Then the train crews would lean out of the cab and grin at the spectacle, and carriage windows would be lowered and flat-capped heads would protrude and ha'-pennies would be thrown in friendly derision to the lonely, striving figure.

'What's your hurry, Jack?'

'Have ye missed the train?'

'Ye've got mixed up, lad. This is the railway track, not the running track.'

Grins and derision and ha'pennies were alike ignored. Anonymous, withdrawn, dedicated, the runner moved in his private world. Other people shared three of the dimensions of that world, but they did not share the fourth. Other people saw a dirty cinder trail stretching along the side of a railway embankment. The runner saw a path leading to glory. I doubt if he got very far along the path. He was one of those who struggled with a barrier in their sprinting. But at least he had a vision beyond the immediate and dreary environment in which he lived and worked. If he couldn't escape from that environment in the flesh, he could escape from it in the spirit. He had experienced the inner challenge. In the course of answering that challenge he would have to pit himself against many other men, but always the most important antagonist he would have to meet was himself. For the other men would be faced in the excitement of competition, but the self had to be overcome in the arduous and monotonous rigours of training.

Training makes, or breaks, the runner. The Latin dramatist Terence wrote a play called the *Self-Tormentor*. It wasn't about an athlete, but with such a title it might well have been. For the self-torment of training is the anvil on which the metal of a runner is shaped and tempered. A man with a good eye may strike a ball well without much practice. P. Mead, the Hampshire cricketer, made a century in his first innings one season, though he hadn't touched a bat since the Scarborough Festival eight months previously. An athlete eight months out of training could not hope to run a good race. But his success or failure will not depend on the amount of actual physical work done in the course of preparation. A factor equally important is the resolution he shows in enduring that preparation, and his refusal to be deterred from it even by the most unlikely and uncongenial surroundings.

According to the late Dr Marie Stopes the best hope for a couple to conceive a perfect child is if the usual preliminaries are carried out in conditions of great natural beauty–a bosky, and suitably secluded, bower in an old-world garden: a herb-scented, sun-caressed slope of the Downs: a lonely and not too sandy cove where the ears of the participants in the rite may be soothed by the murmur of lapping wavelets.

With different intent H. J. Elliott, current holder of the world's mile record, also seeks remote scenes of unspoilt natural charm. Much of his training has been done over the sand dunes and amid the pine woods fringing the eastern coasts of Australia. The object was to make his running as 'natural' and unfettered as is possible for civilised, urbanised man.

The Swedes, with their – to English ears – indelicately-named practice of *fart-lek*, anticipated Elliott's training methods by many years. Two principles are involved in

51

fart-lek (= 'Go as you please'). There is variety in the running, with the athlete going through a sequence of cantering, galloping, 'winders', level ground work and uphill ground work. And the training is done out in the quiet countryside, over rolling grassland, through conifer forests, along the shores of tranquil, reed-fringed lakes. Contemplate beauty, the theory goes, be in contact like Antaeus with mother Earth, and the mind will be refreshed and the body as eager for work as a mustang ranging at will over the wide prairie.

The first practitioners of athletic sports can hardly have failed to draw inspiration from the natural scene around them. Philippides, on his 150 mile run from Athens to Sparta to seek help against the Persians landing at Marathon, even reported that he had met the great god Pan in the wild and desolate mountains of the central Peloponnese, but, *pace* Herodotus, this vision is more likely to have been an offspring of the mirages and noises in the head which afflict the long distance runner than a divine apparition.

The contemporaries of Philippides who took part in more organised athletic occasions saw no visions, but they must have been much affected by the grandeur of the settings wherein their efforts were made, and by the congenial conditions. In Greece the warmth and clarity of the atmosphere invite one to open-air activity, and the challenge of Nature's magnificence awakens that urge to self-expression which may find outlet in building a temple or in pitting one's strength against that of another at quoits. In Greece you are in the world, and yet parts of that world give the impression that they are the threshold of some other region. The stadium at Olympia, situated between the hill of Kronion and the sacred river Alph, had close associations with the near-by sanctuary of the Father of gods and men.

The running which men did there was an aspect of humanity's eternal struggle to reach an understanding with God, or Nature, or however else one chooses to describe the Universal. At Delphi the stadium perches above one of the most sacred and venerated spots in all Hellas, the oracle of Apollo. Here, in truth, was an inspiring place to run.

Take the modern road from Livadia to Delphi and you traverse a route as remote and mysterious as any to be found in a civilised country. For mile after empty mile there is no sign of human dwelling, nor even of human existence. The 8,000-foot bulk of Parnassus hems the road in on the north, while the lower, but still sky-reaching, slopes of Helicon surround it on the south. Here the skin and flesh of the earth have mostly melted away, leaving the bones to show through. It is a stark, lonely country, indifferent to mankind but not actively hostile, fit home for Apollo and the Muses in ancient times, home now only of eagles that sweep low over the traveller as he moves and make him wonder whether they are predators of bigger game than young lambs. The lofty places are all around him, filling him with a sense of insignificance. To arrive at Apollo's Delphic sanctuary is like arriving at the end of this earth, or perhaps at the beginning of another. Silence is here, and drenching light, and a feeling of infinite space as one looks out at mountain vistas, and yet a curious feeling of restriction also, a feeling of being imprisoned by the great rock wall and the gleaming cliffs of the Phaedriades.

In this spot, set well above the sanctuary, carved with great labour out of the flank of Parnassus at a height of over 2,000 feet, lies the stadium where the Pythian Games were held.

For the runner to set foot in such a stadium has much the same emotional effect as would be experienced, say, by a mason if he grubbed through the ruins of a house many thousands of years old and came across hammer and chisel and stone-saw abandoned by an owner who now lies in dust. Here are the tools of his trade, as used by the men who first began to practise it and, with only small difference, as still used by men today. He feels a link across the centuries, across the millennia. The passing of time has not changed us so much after all. To me the desolate stadium, with its narrow length, might be a little unfamiliar in shape, but it was not unfamiliar in purpose. Small thorn bushes sprouted from cracks in the tiers of stone benches and from the stony, sun-baked earth, but men could still run races on this artificial plateau as they had done over two thousand years ago.

Nowadays the runners would be decently, if scantily, covered; in those days they ran naked. But morals were not offended. With the possible exception of a priestess on official duty only men were admitted as spectators. At the far end of the stadium was the finish, with behind it the remains of a triumphal arch. At this curved end (the *sphendone*) a line of stone slabs was let flush into the ground to mark the *aphesis*. Oddly-shaped slots had been sunk into the stones. Their purpose soon became apparent if they were explored with the bare foot. Starting holes and starting blocks were no modern device. The sprinters of ancient Greece placed their toes in these slots so as to get a purchase for the initial drive-off. No doubt, like their modern counterparts, they would sometimes try to gain an advantage over opponents by getting away before the signal. In our case the starter punished 'breaking' by disqualification, should the same man offend twice. More rigorous penalties were enforced in ancient Greece. The judges at Delphi were armed with rods. A 'breaker', being already conveniently unclothed for the chastisement, was flogged on the spot. It must have been a wonderfully effective way of keeping men steady on the 'Get set!'

In settings like this, at Delphi, at Olympia, at Corinth, at Nemea, at Athens, men took part in the first formal athletics competitions which can be historically authenticated. They must have been refreshed by contact with the glories of Nature as much as, if not more than, the Swedes in their forests and Elliott on his sand dunes.

But such settings are not so easy to come by in the modern industrial world. The sooty brick and stone deserts of Clydeside, Tyneside and Merseyside show few examples of noble mountain peaks or undulating grassy swards or rush-bordered lakesides. On the other hand they can furnish an abundance of coke ovens, foundries, shipyards, blast furnaces, machine shops, and pit shafts. These do not make for the contemplation of beauty. In such surroundings a runner gets no assistance from the inspiration of Nature. He must depend on his own resources. The greater credit to him that he is able and willing to do so. A man whose ambition to be a runner is conceived amid the dark, Satanic mills and who labours to attain that ambition against a back-drop of smoke and grime and ugliness earns more merit than the man whose lines are laid in pleasanter places. If the measure of achievement were based only on the number and difficulty of the obstacles to be overcome, the runner sprinting on the railway embankment would rate a high place on the ladder of success.

Elsewhere in Britain of the nineteen-twenties young men, and older men, regularly padded through dingy, gas-lit streets, or past high, forbidding factory walls, or along the towpaths of black, polluted canals, in pursuit not merely of physical fitness but of that elusive, indefinable grail which lures the athlete on. Others of us were luckier and had the use of grammar school playing fields, or cricket grounds, or the sports stadia of works welfare organisations. There are complaints now about the lack of arenas and

55

training facilities for athletes in this country. A generation ago the lack was so gross that few people thought of lamenting it. They did not even seem to notice it. How could you talk of lack of facilities when there were always roads and streets and field-paths available? So long as he has space to move his limbs in, what more should the runner require? Better facilities might persuade more chaps that they had running ambitions, but if a chap had to wait for facilities before taking up running, could he be of much account?

This was the attitude of the old-time road runner, the man who did not seek to exhibit himself on an enclosed track before spectators assembled on tiered stands, the man who performed in obscurity, who did not court fame, who never got his name into the papers. The name 'Harriers' borne by so many of the clubs to which such men belonged indicated that they harked back to a country sport. But by now the country had receded. Hares were rarely started in South Shields or Warrington or Maryhill. Without game to pursue, men still ran. More often than not they were men from poor homes, where the struggle for survival was keen. Yet they could lift their eyes above the struggle, and above the grimness of their environment. Their running wasn't a protest against the environment so much as a conquest of it.

Today, in the sunshine of public favour, track athletics is booming, and even the cross-country men come in for their tribute of newspaper praise. The boom may not last for ever. The clouds of apathy may blot out the sunshine as it has been blotted out in the past. If that happens, it will be the true runner who keeps the sport in being, the man who runs no matter what the facilities available, the man who will, if necessary, create his own facilities and out of the most unlikely material. Other sportsmen need bats and balls and nets and sight screens and prepared pitches and elaborate codes of rules to play their organised games. Th runner doesn't. He requires no apparatus other than a stout heart and a strong pair of legs.

Stoutness of heart, by God, that was necessary sometimes when you had to face the yahoos. In the industrial north a minority of people were interested in and knowledgeable about athletics, a majority were ignorant and indifferent, and a smaller minority were openly derisive of a pursuit so far removed from their own ideas of entertainment. Popular derision is easily borne when you are older and running as one of a pack of harriers. To a lad or youth on his own it can be worse than a knife in the vitals.

At the beginning of my novitiate as a runner, before I was taken seriously at school, someone suggested that if I were in earnest about this business I ought to go out and do some strengthening work on the road. The suggestion seemed a good one. Stamina and strength of muscle would certainly be needed if I hoped to make progress as an athlete. The sight of the local club runners doing their training in winter confirmed that here was a way of developing those desired qualities. But the scheme had its drawbacks. I wasn't yet associated with the local club and therefore my road running would have to be done alone. It was now late spring, so that what the harriers did under cover of a friendly darkness I should have to do in the full light of day. And the most convenient route for me to run over meant that I had to traverse a district where dwelt the type of corner lad with whom in younger days I had been advised not to play.

It was a district on the very outskirts of the town, centring on a coalpit and a railway line, poor but for the most part very respectable. The part that fell short of respectability, to my eyes, at any rate, was a stretch of houses little more than two hundred yards long. It may even have been shorter, for agony seems to be eternal when one passes through it. In the centre of the neighbourhood stood a pub, from which drunken, quarrelling men emerged to strike terror into the scion of a teetotal house. Nearby was a conventicle abandoned by its flock of worshippers and turned into a potato warehouse. But the physical features of the district never made such an impression as did the inhabitants, particularly the younger inhabitants.

They were a tough crowd. The boys wore clothes cut down unskilfully from their fathers' cast-offs. Some went barefoot, some clattered in clogs, which is a footgear not native to the north-east. All had their heads shaved apart from a concessionary fringe above the brow, for nits cannot nest in a cropped skull. The streets were their playground, and they remained in them until late at night, when Father, and perhaps Mother also, returned from the pub. Book learning and the refinements of civilisation they held in small esteem, and those who set store by them in even smaller. But they were good at fighting, and very hardy (they had to be, poor devils), and on election nights the gangs from this quarter terrorised the youth of quieter districts. To do my road work it would be necessary to run the gauntlet of this mob.

The thought made me come out in a sweat. The young love to conform. If there is a section of society with which they cannot, or do not wish to, conform, they keep away from it. Venturing into this den of lions was trial enough when dressed normally and wearing a school cap, for the cap and respectable clothes distinguished you as an outlander, an alien from a different social milieu, one whose pride had to be punctured. With what whoops of derisive glee would the lions greet an outlander clad in exiguous running kit? Dear heaven, it didn't bear thinking of. Fighting the lions understood, and probably football, but running would not be in their world. They would regard running, instinct knew, as a cissy pastime, no fit sport for a lion. And the lions' attitude towards activities in which they had no interest themselves was forthrightly discouraging.

Not a notably intrepid spirit, the doggedness with which I pressed home my first brief programme of road running still amazes. Going out, I couldn't have felt more exposed and vulnerable if I'd been stark naked. The first evening was fine and warm and, alas, in the full blaze of daylight. Trotting over the pavements at the beginning of the run would have been quite enjoyable had it not been for the thought of the ordeal that lay ahead. Some people turned their heads with amusement as I passed, but the amusement was kindly and even approving. One or two children playing with big iron hoops did not let me distract them from their game.

I had to turn a corner and enter a straight stretch of road, mostly lined with lock-up shops, and that straight stretch led into the lions' den. It wasn't possible to enter the den suddenly and bolt through it before the lions could become aware of one's presence. That straight stretch of road had to be negotiated first. Out of the question to make a concealed approach, especially for one bearing the blazon of white vest and shorts. The sentinels would be posted, casually scrutinising oncoming traffic, assessing its entertainment value, looking for the chance to swing on the back of a horse-drawn dray, or to pinch a banana from a barrow, or to whistle at some shy girl and make her blush. Turning the corner, my flesh crawled.

At once hope revived. In the distance the den looked quiet and deserted. Perhaps there was no gauntlet waiting to be run. My pace quickened. Once let me get through this quarter and I was out into open country where lions rarely penetrated. It being Thursday night, the pub was quiet.

59

No urchins loitered about the door of the public bar, seeking a glimpse of their parents whenever the door swung open. I kept my gaze straight ahead, and prayed. Let the little beasts be indoors, or in the back lanes, or playing some dangerous and, with luck, fatal game on the railway track. Here we were now, on the point of entering the lair. No sound, no sight of danger. Only a group of men squatting on their hunkers, pitman style, at a street corner. By heaven, we were getting off scot free!

From a side street, a sudden shout of savage joy which shattered the illusion.

'Hey, look at the runner!'

A clatter of clogs, and then another shout.

'Geordie, look, there's a runner!'

A stifled groan on the part of the runner, and a breaking out of sweat on his brow. The wild beasts were gathering swiftly now, but they were in the rear. Put on a spurt and perhaps they would stay there, noisy but unseen, and therefore the less frightening. Alas, the tumult had brought out other lions from side streets farther ahead.

'Yah, look at the runner coming!'

Bare feet slapped on the flagstones as the neighbourhood came to awful life. Not only out of the side streets did they appear, but apparently out of the ground. Lions everywhere, and what was worse, lionesses. Lions, if the worst came to the worst, could be fought, but civilised opinion said that lionesses could not. One had often wondered that civilised opinion could be so unrealistic.

'Mary Ann, look, it's a runner! He's got nae claes on!'

Faces rose up all around, derisive, jeering, insulting. A scabby mongrel dog snapped at the heels, delighted for once to find that someone else's life was being made a misery. Urchins sprinted alongside, mocking the runner's strides with their own exaggerated leg movements. The noise of hooting rose in the mean street like the beating of giant wings. It was a torment of the soul far more bitter than any torture of the body. And through it all one had to run with measured step, eyes fixed ahead as if unaware of the tumult, trying to abolish it by ignoring it.

That measured step cost much in effort. Instincts were screaming to break into a mad sprint and fight a way out of this mobbing. When bodies jostled or feet were thrust out with intent to trip, there was a temptation to strike blindly with the fists, careless of whether crop-headed males or lank-haired females were the target. But the temptation had to be resisted. Physical violence by one against the mob would only result in the one getting a severe mauling. More than that, physical violence would be an acknowledgment that the commotion was distressing, and such acknowledgment would be more than halfway to admitting that one had been defeated by it. If the mob couldn't be outfaced this once, it could never be outfaced at all. The lions had to learn to accept the fact that one intended to become a runner. Blustering and fighting would not teach them to accept it. Such conduct would only bring the runner down to their level, which was where they wanted to have him. So long as their existence was ignored they weren't quite sure of themselves, didn't quite know whether or not to make the final, fatal spring. So carry on. Puzzle them by pretending that nothing unusual is happening. Endure this long enough and often enough and the lions will eventually tire of the entertainment and look elsewhere for sport.

But it is a hard thing for youth to set itself alone against spite and hostility. I did that run a number of times, and never faced it without a premonitory chill of the spine. Having stood the jeers to the point where I could persuade myself I wasn't giving up through cowardice, I quietly abandoned the practice.

CHAPTER FIVE

MY BRIEF APPEARANCE in the role of Daniel took place when I was about fifteen. At that age I was much too old for scholars' races at local handicap meetings, but not quite old enough for serious junior competition. It was a betwixt and between period, the period when a boy frets because he has the ambition to play a man's part but not the ability or the knowledge. To be a runner was still the object, but it took a painfully long time to realise it.

At sixteen they seemed to regard me as having crossed the invisible line separating boyhood from youth. I started formal training. It was rapture. The very word 'training' had an almost mystic significance. Although it was aimed only at the junior sprint championships of Northumberland and Durham, I regarded the work as an act of dedication. I was the novice preparing to take his vows, the esquire doing night-long vigil in the chapel before receiving the accolade, the sorcerer's apprentice about to be initiated into the mysteries of the black arts. A fellow had to be worthy to be a runner, and he proved his worth beforehand by a suitable sacrifice of toil and sweat. School-fellows might bowl or bat lightheartedly at the cricket nets, or play a desultory game of tennis. I slogged round and round the Rugby football pitch, doing a stated stint of laps, or sprinted against myself across the field.

For a while, I was the only one of my generation at school to be badly bitten by the running bug. Thus my self-imposed ordeal tended to mark me off from other fellows who took their pleasures less savagely. I was happy so to be marked off. By one still two years away from adult competition the business may seem to have been taken too seriously, but I don't think so. To declare an intention early in life is a great strengthener of the purpose. As you grow up you grow into the chosen pursuit. You must discern your target clearly if you hope to hit it. My target was to be an even-time sprinter.

Enthusiasm carried me through the first few weeks of that summer's training, the excitement of at last having my feet set on the golden road to Samarkand. But I soon found it wasn't enough just to set your feet on the road, you had to keep moving them. That was a more arduous affair than seeing visions or discerning targets. Once the glamour had gone only the hard work remained. Even to an athlete hard work sometimes palls.

Two main temptations lie in wait for the runner who has planned a training season of so many evenings or afternoons of work per week, for so many weeks or months. The first temptation, when one of those afternoons or evenings comes along, is not to spend it in running. It may seem preferable to the runner to post up his stamp collection, or go to the cinema, or even do preparation for the morrow's lessons. Surely to miss training just this once won't matter? After all, there's a long season of it lying ahead. But conscience wags a finger. Conscience points out that to miss training once is to open a breach in the wall of routine. And a single breach will almost certainly be followed by others, to the point where there is no routine left. And then bang goes your ambition to be a runner. Once you have got into the habit of enduring torment you must not get out of it.

A temptation more insidious is to cut a training session short after it has been started. This is insidious because you try to convince yourself you've earned merit merely by turning out, without needing to go through the whole gamut of toil. Such a dishonest suggestion is not always easy to counter, especially if you're a sprinter doing donkey work for the sake of gaining strength. To practise starts or do striding runs or break into flat-out sprints, such work is welcome. Its object is immediately apparent, and you like doing it anyway because it's your special function. What you don't like at all is the preparatory grind of jogging endlessly round a track at the beginning of a season after a long lay-off, when the only object in the running is to get your body used to the idea of running.

The labour is monotonous and distasteful. You start off on the first lap or two briskly enough, with your legs moving lightly and your breath coming easily. You say to yourself this is going to be no bother at all. You soon change your mind.

An ache develops round the ankles, or in the calves or shins, as muscles and tendons protest against an ill-treatment which they haven't experienced for some time. All right, you ignore the ache. Possibly, if you're feeling savage with yourself, you even step up the pace a little so that the muscles can have a taste of real ill-treatment. The aching passes and is replaced by a numbness which indicates that the muscles are still far from happy about the situation but have abandoned further protest as useless. But now the body registers a more serious objection to this exercise it has been dragooned into. The lower limbs begin to feel heavy as fatigue products build up in them. The physiological process of muscle break-down under stress is a complicated one, but complex or simple the effect upon the runner is the same. His legs feel like lumps of lead. It takes a much greater effort to lift them and push them forward and pick them up. The burden of carrying the body along is something they revolt from. They want rest, they groan for rest, they will seize up and refuse to move at all if they are driven any harder.

By now the runner's respiratory system will be making its protest. Breathing has become laboured. The lungs pant as they strive to take in more air to oxygenate the blood which the pounding heart pumps round to the overworked limbs. If only the gaping mouth can take in enough oxygen the fatigue products in the legs will be at least partially dissipated and some of this inertness will lift. But you can't take in enough oxygen. You've only just started training. Your system isn't used to effort. The dead weight in your legs remains. You have to learn to live with it, move with it. Your mouth is dry and bitter-tasting. Whatever it may be normally, now it's only a suction funnel, gulping in gas. Clammy sweat trickles down your face and body. The tiredness has descended upon your arms. You drive them forward in a pumping motion, trying to force yet more air into your bellows. But you find that the extra energy required for the arm-drive is subtracted from the energy available for the legs. Your body is a desert of weariness.

And all the time your mind thoroughly disapproves of the whole, mad, damnable exercise. Or rather, one part, the civilised part, disapproves, and asks why in God's name the stupidity can't be stopped. The other part, more rugged and primitive, tells civilisation to shut up and, if it can't make a positive contribution to the work in hand, at least not to sabotage it.

The run becomes a battle fought out at staff head-quarters between the reason and the will, while the limbs, lower down, endure the agony to which they have been committed by a pig-headed commander.

Perhaps twelve quarter-mile laps have been laid down as the training stint. In a body out of training the fatigue will develop long before six laps have been done. Stop it now, urges Staff Captain Reason. Enough has been done in proof of endeavour. The rest of the job can be left for another day. Lieutenant-Colonel Will shakes his head. A task has been started. That task must be finished. You know what happens to tasks that are put off till another day. Now look, he says, turning to the legs, carry on just a little further. We're coming up to the finish of the sixth lap now. That's half the grind over. Now, pretend that for this first half of the distance you've been struggling uphill, but now there's an easier downhill run in front of you. You know damn well it isn't easier? That's enough insubordination. I said pretend it was easier. You've run round the track so often you can now pick out every blade of grass? Good. If you count them you'll be too busy to think of your other troubles.

Now while you were arguing, you did a lap. That's seven you've completed. Only five left. Well done, legs. Well done, body. Of course you don't want to pack up now. It would be a shame, with not much more than a third of the run left to do. Why not vary the monotony a bit? Don't keep your arms tucked up like that, but drop them straight down and swing them stiffly. It makes a change. It sees you a few yards farther on your way. Every stride you take brings you nearer home. Imagine you're a horse perking up when its head is turned towards the stable. What's that? Never mind the bloody stable? You've had enough of this? You're going to stop? By God, you're not. Not while I'm in charge. There you are, a mere four laps to go. Remember this is a strengthening exercise. You can't hope for the strength if you don't do the work. Persuade yourself you're just starting out, with no more than a paltry mile to run. What's a mile compared with the two miles you've already covered?

Good show, legs. Soon it'll be only three laps, and then two, and then one. The milestones will have reeled off.

When it's over you know very well you'll be glad you stuck it. Sense of achievement more than makes up for weariness and discomfort. Fatigue is soon forgotten, but failure isn't. What did you say? You think it might be an idea to take a little breather now and knock off the three laps you owe later on? Nothing doing. No breathers. It's the perseverance that counts. One prolonged effort is more testing and effective than any number of shorter efforts. Come on. You're within sight of home. Two laps to go. A mere trifle. Tuck this second last lap under your belt and you'll hardly notice the very last circuit. Yes, yes, of course it's agony, but the agony is nearly done with. Soon that intolerable weight will be lifted from the legs, and the lungs will cease to sob, and the sky will no longer be dark in front of the eyes.

You're practically there. You're on the last lap. Now, show them what you're made of. Show them you're not half dead. Drive yourself. Hold off that weakness for just a few seconds longer. Stop your knees buckling. Keep your shoulders straight. *Sprint in!*

All runners, whether good or bad, feel something like that while in motion. The first stage of the run is comparatively easy, then the man begins to ask why he submitted himself to this painful ordeal, then comes the even more difficult question of why the hell he doesn't stop it. But he never does stop, not unless he's ill. Once you start a stint of training you must keep going, you must finish it. Not to finish it would have a bad psychological effect. You wouldn't want to give up halfway through a race, therefore you mustn't give up halfway through a training run. Giving up can become a habit, and not a good one.

The basic stuff of training is a bed of nails on which the runner shifts uneasily. One year, I remember, my appetite for self-torment was so great that I decided the nails weren't sharp enough. If suffering made the runner, then didn't it seem logical that the more the suffering the better the runner? So instead of training in comparative comfort at the end of school or on sports afternoons I determined that the true devotee of running would rise early, spurning the habit of staying in bed (to which I was much addicted) and go out to do his work when the day was fresh and new.

It happened, at the time when I reached this conclusion, that the mornings were not only fresh and new but also unpleasantly cold. Winter was late departing that year. Showers of sleet and a bitter east wind greeted me as I set off from home through grey, silent streets and made for a meadow not far from the farm track where I first knew competitive running. Shivering, I stripped off outdoor things and emerged in vest and shorts. The long grass of the meadow was soaking wet. One half of me was asleep, the other half numbed with cold. In the distance the bleak walls of the lunatic asylum reared against the gloomy sky, an appropriate setting for my efforts.

'The year's at the spring, and day's at the morn,' I assured myself between chattering teeth.

But there was no lark on the wing, only a foolish youth sprinting backwards and forwards over a 150 yard stretch of melancholy field. Ruminating cows watched me curiously. One or two workers on their way to catch an early train stopped and gazed over the rail with wondering sympathy. At the end of the exercise I had no sense of euphoria, no feeling that the blood was coursing redly through my veins, no belief that all was right with the world. Contrary to adult advice I persisted in these performances for some time until I caught cold and developed pleurisy. Enthusiasm can be taken too far, reluctant though I am to make such a statement about running.

A runner who trains alone may do so out of necessity

Often enough it will be because he wants to. Like a bride coy about being seen in her night attire he prefers that his period of preparation should go unwitnessed. The ugly, distressing stages of his evolution towards race-fitness are no more for the public eye than the early rehearsals of a stage company, who go through their lines in ordinary clothes, with no properties on the stage, carpenters hammering somewhere at the back, and the producer cutting in every few moments to tell them how awful they are. The actor, and the runner, want to put the finished article before the public, not the crude beginnings. The public is quite content with this, the Press not always.

R. G. Bannister incurred the displeasure of certain newspapers because he preferred to practise in private instead of before an audience of news reporters and television cameras. He also preferred to keep his training methods secret. Since Bannister's running had considerable news value at the time, the attitude annoyed those Pressmen who feel that their occupation gives them the right to probe into every aspect of an interesting subject's life and behaviour. But each individual's training is his own affair. It is not criticism of that which he invites, but of his performance when he finally steps into the arena.

Sometimes, reading articles in the Press or books on athletics, one gets the impression that serious training for running is a post-war invention. We're so much more systematic now, one is assured, more scientific. We prepare our men in accordance with nicely calculated schedules. Look at these training schemes for Kuts or Pirie or Jungwirth. That's the way to produce an athlete. Give him plenty of work, carefully graded, carefully sorted, carefully arranged, so that at half-past three in the afternoon twelve months from now he'll know whether it's time to blow his nose or to run 5,000 metres.

Strong men lived before Agamemnon. Training schedules were not handed down with the Tablets of the Law on top of Mount Sinai, to be later lost sight of and only recently disinterred with the Dead Sea scrolls. No magic inheres in a training schedule. Two different coaches would produce two different schedules for the same runner. Sometimes the slavish following of schedules can be an indication that the runner isn't able to think for himself. I cannot recall that A. G. K. Brown, Lord Burghley, E. H. Liddell or W. R. Applegarth made much use of such formularies. The days of those old-time distance men A. Shrubb and W. G. George were innocent of scientific preparation. Their running did not seem to suffer.

Those men of former generations and plenty of men of the modern generation could and can estimate their own training requirements by testing themselves against the watch or against the opposition of club-mates. It is obvious that if they hope to run fast in competition, they must previously run fast in training. If a distance man finds he has no 'drive' over the last lap, he must sharpen himself with speed work, while if he cannot cope with the pace set by opponents then he is short of strength. Having analysed his defects he will set about remedying them on his own initiative, very likely with help and advice but without asking for a set of documents specifying in detail his athletics activities and, for all I know, the working of his metabolism, for the next six months.

To be told what to do can be a great relief. The chores are set, and if they are done the runner has his adviser's assurance that his ability will have been developed to the full. And it is no mean achievement to stick to some of the gruelling training programmes drawn up by modern distance coaches. Given judicious publicity they can even frighten the opposition. But to me it is a greater achievement if a man shoulders the responsibility for himself, if he decides what he needs to do to win an Olympic title, and then goes out and does it. All runners need advice and comfort at times. Some runners get to the point of relying on advice as a cripple relies on a crutch. They finish up by playing Galatea to the coach's Pygmalion.

In field events the case is not the same. Here a difficult technique may have to be learnt, and the instruction of a coach may prevent a man from making too many confusing and time-wasting errors. The coach is the repository of other men's achievements and advances in the particular event. He can give his pupil a good start by hoisting him on to those men's shoulders. Even so, technical advances in an event are not as a rule made by the coach but by the men performing it.

The outstanding recent development in shot-putting is the step-back technique, with which P. O'Brien of the United States achieved his ambition to be the first man to cast the 16 lb. weight a distance of 60 feet. Unable to reach his goal by any orthodox approach, O'Brien, as it were, turned his back on the problem. It occurred to him that he should be able to do a better cast if he turned away from the line of putt and executed a full 180-degree curve in the process of thrusting the shot forward and upward. An elementary principle of mechanics lay behind the idea, that the longer he pushed the shot, applying force against a moving object, the longer the throw would be.

O'Brien's discovery is interesting in itself, and also for the reactions it evoked from athletics coaches.

'I was criticised by German and other experts,' O'Brien said, 'because they did not think it natural for the body to move in such a way. My adviser, Jesse Mortensen, approved the idea, but it was such a new idea that I had to be my own coach, with Mortensen merely picking out the

71

rough spots. Other coaches said I would never get any-where.'

Now the step-back technique is standard practice for the shot-putter, and appears in all the coaching handbooks. The point is not made to decry coaches, and the long, devoted service many of them give to athletics, but to warn a prospective track or field man that he will not find success by relying entirely on the teaching of another. The athlete is captain of the ship, with the coach as pilot. Sometimes, in the ship's best interests, it will be necessary for the captain to ignore the pilot's advice.

In my first year at Cambridge two or three of us, fresh-men, and track runners, thought we would vary the labour of track training by doing some field events work. Hesitantly we asked if we might receive instruction in throwing the javelin, an event not yet included in the programme for the Varsity Sports. Alec Nelson, the C.U.A.C. coach, did not pretend to know anything about this outlandish Conti-nental sport, and a senior man, F. R. Webster, the pole vaulter, kindly offered to take us in hand. I repeat it was kind of him, and yet I think he went about the instruction the wrong way. Instead of putting a practice javelin in our hands, marking out a scratch line, and then saying, 'Go on, throw the bloody thing,' Webster was determined that from the very beginning we should learn the 'correct' technique.

In the middle nineteen-thirties the Finns were pre-eminent in the javelin, and it was the throwing technique practised by the leading Finnish exponents (which he had mastered) that Webster tried to teach us. This involved an elaborate arm drill to bring the javelin from a kind of 'present' position to the throwing position, accompanied by some even more intricate footwork as one came up to the scratch line. We listened unhappily as these peculiar

72

movements were explained to us. Webster made it all sound so hellish difficult. And it was a needless difficulty. A technique evolved for themselves by leading Finns, no doubt over many years, was not in the least necessary for raw beginners who only wanted to do some throwing as a change from running. Even had we had ambitions about becoming first-class javelin men, there was still no need for us to follow this 'correct' Finnish technique. There is no universal 'correct' technique. That technique is best which projects the javelin farthest.

In 1938, a couple of years after I had given up my own endeavours in the event, I watched J. F. Klein of the C.U.A.C. throw a, for those days, perfectly satisfactory 191 feet 10 inches in the Varsity Sports. He did so by running up to the line with his javelin held in arm stretched out straight behind him, and then bringing the arm through and over with whiplash speed and power. The motions were quite simple. What made them effective was their co-ordination, and the force behind them. This was not put into Klein by coaching, but by assiduous practice and study.

In 1956 an ingenious Spaniard discovered that by spinning round after the fashion of a discobolos, instead of making the orthodox approach run, he could cast the javelin beyond the magic 300 feet. Unhappily he could not be sure where his cast would go, and the I.A.A.F. banned this method on the grounds of possible damage to spectators, and also because the sports stadia of the world would have had to be lengthened at great cost to contain these phenomenally long throws. Not wishing to labour a point, one might add that it was an athlete, not a coach, who thought up this unusual method.

The greatest benefit which a coach can confer on a pupil is not technical instruction but (especially in the case of a track man) mental comfort and support. For sometimes the runner's loneliness becomes almost unbearable. Then he falls into doubts about his capacity, or becomes wearied of striving if the striving brings no reward. At such a time it can give a great fillip to the spirits to know that there is at least one other person as anxious about your welfare as you are yourself. That anxiety may be expressed by soothing words and a lump of sugar, or by a crack of the whip.

On me, when I was at school, Spuggy mostly used the whip.

He was short, well-muscled, auburn-haired, and very alert in his movements. In Tyneside *patois* 'Spuggy' means a sparrow. The nickname suited him. Despite his modest stature he wasn't a man to trifle with. In the gymnasium he assured us that no exercise ever did any good until it hurt. He took good care that it did hurt. Apocryphal tales spread of a boy breaking his spine as he forced his body back at an ever more unnatural angle under the spur of Spuggy's invective. In class Spuggy was an efficient performer with the rod, having formulated a theory that the effectiveness of a caning depended on the 'follow-through' of the arm, as in a golf drive or cricket stroke. The executioner should aim, he would inform an apprehensive class, not at the victim's person but through it. He put the theory into practice with evident satisfaction to himself. Those at the receiving end showed less appreciation.

As a road runner I think Spuggy always retained some contempt for those exhibitionists who sought to perform on a track before the plaudits of the multitude. Certainly he showed no great interest when I told him I wanted to extend my running activities outside the walls of school.

'Do you? What for?'

'Well, sir, I'd like to become a decent sprinter.'

'And how would you define a decent sprinter?'

'I suppose a chap who can do evens, sir.'

74

'You want to do evens, is that your idea?'

'Yes, sir.'

'So do ten thousand others. However.'

He went on to give me details of the two championship events which at that age I was qualified to enter for, and then started to walk away.

'But, sir,' I appealed, 'what do you think I should do? I mean, how does a chap become a good runner?'

'How do you become a good runner?' Spuggy stared at me in amazement. 'Why, boy, you simply get out on the field there and run! You run till you drop. Then you get up and run some more!'

Later I learnt from other fellows, especially those who had been at Rutlish, that they were given elaborate training schedules to follow by their games masters. Spuggy never gave me any schedules. He didn't want me to get the idea that success in running could come from slavishly conforming with a course of conduct prescribed by someone else. He believed that in the end a runner would do far better if obliged to think for himself. And if he refused to think for himself, then plainly the boy, or man, wasn't worthy to be a runner. Train until you thought you were ready for competition, was his idea, and then take part in it. If the competition revealed certain weaknesses, go back to training and eradicate them. Then offer yourself for competition once more. The process was one of trial and error. Let the runner make his own mistakes, and afterwards profit by them. If I did anything blatantly wrong or stupid, he would tell me. Otherwise he left me to get on with it. There was never any checking to ensure that I got through a regular stint of training. The responsibility for doing the work was mine alone.

Spuggy gave me little encouragement, even when my extra-mural adventures in running were successful. He soon detected that I had a tendency towards self-satisfaction when things went well. He did no more than look casually when I showed him the first gold medal I won.

'How do you think I'm getting on, sir?' I asked.

The expected answer was, 'Brilliantly, my boy,' or 'Quite phenomenally,' or 'You show every sign of becoming a first-class sprinter'.

The actual answer was, 'You're doing about as well as most boys who win the junior county championship, but not so well as some.'

'But, sir, I won it and I'm only sixteen.'

'If you'd won it when you were fifteen there might have been something to boast about.'

The dusty answer annoyed me. So Spuggy didn't think much of my running? Then I would show him. There were the two county sprint championships this year, and the same two next year, and after that the wider fields of area and national championships. Good performances in these couldn't be passed over indefinitely. At some point Spuggy was going to have to admit that I was a decent runner, a sprinter of even-time potential. I went out on to the playing fields and worked grimly, driving myself hard in training, determined to earn commendation from the one person who didn't seem disposed to give it. Only later did I realise that, had his attitude been different, I might not have driven myself.

Further successes came. Spuggy affected to regard them with no greater enthusiasm. Instead of victories it might have been a dead cat that I'd thrust under his nose. Some time after my venture, other boys in the school had begun to take running seriously. With them, Spuggy spent quite a lot of time, giving encouragement, patiently watching them trundle round the field, advising them as to the events for which he thought they were best fitted. By comparison my own activities hardly received notice.

Jealously I commented on the fact.

'Perhaps I spend a lot of time on the others because I think they're worth it,' Spuggy said.

'Which means you think I'm not?'

'I never said so.'

'It's damned unfair.' I had reached an age where I thought I could bandy words with a master. 'For two years I've worked hard and I've done pretty well, or at least everyone else says so. But you just take what I've done as a matter of course.'

'If you've got the approval of the world at large, you don't need mine as well, do you?'

Sullenly I went off. I did need his approval. Important events lay ahead, events well outside my range of experience so far. Good conceit though I might have of myself, it would be a great help, in facing those events, to know that I had his confident backing. He was a man with knowledge of this bigger world of running that I was about to enter. I trusted his judgment. I didn't expect him to say that he thought I'd win, but what I did hope to hear was the expressed belief that I would do well, that I would respond to these imminent challenges.

Well, it looked as if I would have to meet the challenges without such moral support.

Shortly afterwards one of the fellows junior to me won the under-eighteen county championship for which I was no longer eligible. The feat was announced at morning assembly. The fellow displayed his medal to interested parties. I saw and heard Spuggy admiring it. So the favouritism at last was being openly expressed. The other fellow rated higher in his estimation than I did. Youth does not take such a discovery easily, but what was there to do except bite on the bullet?

Later in the day I raised the matter with Spuggy, trying to speak casually.

'So-and-so did very well.'

'Yes, indeed, better than I expected.'

'Next year, I suppose, you'll be entering him for the area and national championships?'

'Good heavens, no.'

'But why not?'

'Because I don't think he'd stand a chance.'

'But – but,' I struggled to adjust myself to an unexpected situation, 'but you've entered me for them this year.'

'That's right.'

'Which – which must mean that you think I do stand a chance?'

'It seems an obvious inference.'

'Oh.' Understanding was beginning to come, a realisation that what appeared on the surface didn't always reflect what went on underneath. After all, Spuggy did think I might do well. The sense of relief was great. 'I didn't know. I mean, I thought you had a different idea.'

'Well, your idea was wrong.'

'So you really think I'm good enough for the Northern Counties and the 3 A's?'

'God Almighty, boy, do you want me to set it to music?'

CHAPTER SIX

SCRATCH A RUSSIAN and you'll find a Tartar. You don't need to scratch a runner to find an individualist.

Concerning other sportsmen you may often hear the comment passed or the epitaph composed – 'Good old Tom (or Dick), he always fought hard for his team.' Had Tom (or Dick) been a runner the comment would have to be phrased, 'Good old Tom, he always fought hard for himself.'

This self-interest of Tom's and of others like him does not always make them well-loved by their fellow-creatures. Much of life is a common struggle towards a common goal. The runner opts out of this. He is a non-co-operator. He feels no desire to submerge his individuality in a larger whole for the general good. His view of the good is much more narrow than that. Victory on the cricket or Rugby field is shared by eleven or fifteen men. In a hundred yards sprint it is only one man who feels that brief pull of the worsted across his chest which tells him he's won. With six men in the race the odds, mathematically, are five to one against it being your chest that breaks the worsted. Taking into account the competition histories of the other runners the odds may be even higher. Never mind. The runner prefers to accept the considerable risk of defeat for the sake of the slender chance of solitary victory. Except in relay racing a shared win is not to his liking.

'Friend is friend,' an entrepreneur of alien origin once said to me, 'but business is business.'

Running is the athlete's business. He conducts it with no partners. Friends, club-mates, coach, these do not count as partners. The runner would happily push them all under a train if he thought the mass slaughter would expedite his winning of an Olympic title.

It is no accident that the ancient Greeks were the first practitioners of organised athletics, for no more individualistic people than the Greeks has ever existed, whether in ancient or modern times ('Show me five Greeks and I'll show you six Prime Ministers'). Team pursuits have never been to their taste, not even war, much though they have indulged in the latter and much though they have suffered defeat through their refusal to combine and co-operate. Our present-day Marathon race commemorates the victory of a single Greek city over the might of the Persian Empire, a victory won while the rest of Hellas looked on and did nothing. One versus the Rest, that is something to fire the imagination, the struggle of a single champion to assert his absolute supremacy in a contest over all others. In a hundred yards sprint or in a 20 miles road race there is only one first place. All the rest is defeat. Silver or bronze may console defeat. Victory is acclaimed with gold.

If these remarks suggest that the runner is a person of no marked generosity of temper, that, on the track, is quite true. Ask any man who has been one of a field of twelve fighting to get the inside position at the first bend in a half-mile race. The runners give nothing away, make no chivalrous gestures to an opponent. No quixotism here. Too much is at stake. The performers have had to endure a long period of hard and monotonous work to bring themselves to the pitch of competition-fitness. Now, out on the track, they will be very conscious that anything achieved will depend entirely on their own muscles, their own lung-power, their own resolution. Self-help is the first law of the jungle. No one else is going to help you.

In that field of twelve for the half-mile, no man is a friend. You are encompassed about by enemies. That sportsmanlike shaking of hands before the start, those insincere expressions of good wishes, meant nothing. The same hand which took yours with such a firm grip may be the first to give you an impatient push if the owner thinks you are unduly obstructing his progress. Eleven bodies are striving, and the object of their strife is you. Even more hostile than the bodies are the minds, reaching out towards yours, thinking how you can be bested, trying to establish a moral ascendancy over you, calculating whether a fast first quarter will draw your sting and leave you trailing at the rear, or whether to run the first circuit more slowly and then leave you with a searing finishing sprint over the last furlong. Imagine you are in such a contest. You counter hostility with hostility, driving up on the back straight into third place, a good position to strike from when the time comes.

Oh, God, three of your rivals have suddenly come up and boxed you in on this second bend. They've combined to box you in not because they have any love for each other but because for the moment their hostility towards you gives them a common purpose. They've boxed you in, and the two leaders are beginning to draw away as the first lap is finished. If you don't go after them now they'll establish such an advantage that you won't be able to catch them. But these brutes are deliberately slowing you down. You've got to get out of the box. Yet how can you, with one man immediately ahead, so near that his spikes are almost gashing your shins, and the other two at your shoulder and at your heels?

You could get out of the box by decelerating and dropping to the rear, but that would mean an undesirable break in speed and a loss of yards. Probably your opponents would then move up shoulder to shoulder, facing you with a living wall, forcing you to run right outside them with a further loss of yards. Panting breath and spikes crackling in the cinders is all the noise you hear. Somewhere remote in the distance the crowd are shouting, but you don't care about the crowd. You only care about these arms and legs flying all round you. Move, you bastards, move! All right, if you want a punch in the kidneys, here it comes.

Blast, you've stayed in the box too long. You've got no hope of catching the leaders now. The man in front is fifteen yards up on you. Fifteen yards, and you're on the second lap with less than four hundred yards to go. You can't make up fifteen yards in less than four hundred, not with the fatigue engendered by the first quarter already beginning to weigh you down. You stupid fool, you let them fox you. The leaders are coming back as you make your effort, but they're not coming back quickly enough. At least you can beat these tykes who kept you shut in the box, but what use is that? You've lost the race. You let the enemy get the upper hand of you. You didn't view them at the start with enough determination and hatred. Their minds reached out and caught your mind in a moment of indecision and imposed their will on it. You forgot the first rule of the track, which is that on it there are no friends. You must never let up, never look for any quarter from the opposition, never cease to assert yourself physically and morally.

We, who perform, may prefer to call it individualism. Others, who watch, may term it less favourably as egoism.

The obvious danger in an activity where a man stands or falls entirely by his own efforts is that a large measure of success may make him conceited. Many runners have not avoided this danger. It is the reverse side of the medal of their individualism. In team games a man can also have a large opinion of himself, but even the most notable cricketer or footballer has to admit that his success is due in part to the other ten or fourteen men in the side, if only because without them there wouldn't even be a game. The runner need make no such concession. He alone stands on the victory dais or goes to the prize table, and it is his name which appears in the record books. His success is individual and personal.

So is his defeat.

Again the comparison with team games is illuminating. When a cricket or Rugby football team plays poorly, the blame of failure is shared among eleven or fifteen men. A defeated runner carries the whole blame of failure himself. In a race where a man can have had no reasonable expectation of winning, blame is too strong a word to use. No more than a measure of disappointment is felt, and this may well be alleviated if the runner's performance in the event is the best he has done so far. But to lose a race where you expected to win, where you hoped with all your heart to win, that is to know bitterness.

You have to go up to the winner, who is smiling broadly at his victory, and offer him congratulations. You have to watch other people offering him congratulations. He is the man of the moment. You are merely an also ran. Depression lies heavy upon you. You view the track with loathing. You have a feeling as if you'd stepped confidently through an open doorway and, instead of setting foot on some ample terrace or spacious gallery, had fallen into a black, empty void. There are ashes in your mouth and nausea in your stomach. Yet again you marvel that defeat in a race can so alter the complexion of life, can so plunge a man into the deeps of despair.

Perhaps someone comes up and gives a casual pat of consolation on the shoulder. The difference between that casual, off-hand pat for the loser, and the excited handshake which would have been your meed as the winner, is too poignant to contemplate.

83

'Bad luck,' someone else offers, hurrying over to have a word with the chap who beat you.

But there's the rub. If you thought it was bad luck, or plain inferior ability, that caused your defeat, you would be more willing to accept it. But there was no bad luck about it, nor any marked difference in ability. If anything, the advantage should have lain with you. You and he were both sprinters, running in the same class of competition. You had never met each other over a furlong before, but comparing performances against other opposition you seemed to have the edge. Your best time for the distance was point two of a second better than his. Point two of a second is two yards, which may not sound much but looks, and is, a lot. That was the amount you should have beaten him by. Instead, he beat you, only by a foot, but it might as well have been by the length of the home straight.

Dear God, why can't the race be run again? Next time you would know better. Next time you would do better. But the race is never run again, not in fact, though you will run it again many times over in your mind. For days that re-running will go on, even for weeks, taking place at the most unlikely moments, distracting your mind from the ledger you may be casting up or the cylinder head you may be machining or the diagram of a frog's sexual apparatus which you may be chalking up on the blackboard.

You see the six men getting down to their marks, settling their feet in the holes, or, if it be a post-war vision, on the blocks. This time you're much more confident. You know where you made the mistake. Your idea was to keep something in reserve as you went round that tight White City bend and then really pull the stops out as you entered the straight. But the half-hearted opening dash put you at a disadvantage. The other fellow went away at full steam By the time you came out of the bend he'd established a two-yard lead. It was too big a lead to cut down. His advantage was established, concrete, factual, whereas the advantage you'd counted upon, of having a little extra steam in the boiler, was only potential. That potential couldn't be realised. Mentally you had blunted yourself. You opened the throttle, but there was no instant pick-up of speed. He was out there in front, plainly visible. The lead had given him confidence, but it worried you, began to make you struggle and 'tie up'. There are times when the tape seems a mile away, but this time, damnation, it was too near. Now he was coming back at you as he tired, but you were tiring as well. The judges were squinting along the line of the finish. Only another ten yards and you might have done it. But the ten yards weren't given. The moving finger had already written. The pull of the worsted wasn't felt across your chest, but across his.

Now, in your vision, you know better. At the gun you leave your holes fast, as fast as you know how. You have the inside lane while he is in number 2, the stagger giving him an apparent advantage of nearly four yards. Almost at once you're into the bend and you know you're going well. There's nothing half-hearted about this opening burst. You're putting your heart into it, and your strength, and yet you feel the movement is easy and relaxed. He's coming back, of course, since the stagger is unwinding to your advantage, but surely he's coming back faster than that would justify? By God, he is. Over the crown of the bend and you're level with him now. Suddenly he disappears. You've pulled past him! You're into the straight now with a clear lead over him and a clear run through to the tape. You're gloriously alone. The feet padding behind you aren't coming any nearer. They may even be falling back. That's the finish, with the judges crouching down to squint along the tape. You're winning the race which you should have won!

Suddenly it isn't a tape which you're looking at, but a ledger, or a cylinder head, or a blackboard. You didn't win that race. No matter how many times you re-run it in your head, the stark, factual, cruel result remains the same.

The runner is an egoist? Yes. But he suffers for it.

The bitterness of defeat depends partly on the extent to which the runner has contributed to his own downfall, and partly on the importance which he and others attach to the contest. To fail in the Olympics is a more dreadful thing than to fail at the Coalpit Colliery Sports, unless the Coalpit Sports are the very butt and sea mark of your utmost ambition.

In this respect a boy is in a happier position than a man. He is willing to take a race as it comes, on its merits, without concerning himself too much whether it is a county championship or a conflict of lesser degree. The prospect of the race will excite him beforehand, but it isn't likely to worry him. Worry is not yet in his nature. His experience is too limited. There must be a basis for comparison before a person can worry, a knowledge of the standards that can be expected to apply to him. When the time comes, the boy will strive mightily, knowing happiness if the striving succeeds and disappointment if it fails. But neither happiness nor disappointment will be long-lived. Perhaps memory, with its peculiar selective faculty, will even forget early triumphs and keep more vivid record of later disasters.

News of insignificant events and insignificant persons can be bruited abroad quite surprisingly even in a conurbation of a million souls. In 1933 informed circles on the banks of the Tyne and Wear had decided (on what evidence I still cannot imagine) that the two chief contenders for the Northumberland and Durham junior sprint championships were L. Duns and myself. Duns was a stocky boy with

air skin and flaming red hair. Later he became a professional footballer and I saw him play on the right wing for
Sunderland in 1937 when they beat Preston North End
–1 in the Cup Final at Wembley. I think he was some
months older than my sixteen years, which accounts for the
fact that he couldn't turn out in the junior championships
of the following year.

Of the first encounter with Duns I remember nothing,
either where it took place nor what sort of contest we had.
Presumably I won it since I have the gold medal awarded
to the 100 yards title-holder, the medal which Spuggy
viewed with such unconcern. Our second encounter is as
clear in the memory as if it had taken place last week.

The second race was one of the events on the programme
of the Newcastle Police Sports, held at St James's Park, the
Newcastle United football ground (County championship
events are usually farmed round to different sports meetings instead of being run through on one programme). St
James's Park is the only stadium I have ever known where
they laid down an absolutely square track. In the furlong
it wasn't a question of us coping with two sharp curves, but
with two right-angled corners. There were no lanes, and
eight of us were included in the final. It could be foreseen
that some interesting situations would develop at the start
of the race.

Neither Duns nor I took much notice of the other
finalists. This wasn't arrogance, but a calm conviction that
the race lay between us. One of my school-fellows was
among the eight, a fair-haired, keen-faced boy who looked
a fine, stylish runner when you saw him in solitary training
but who didn't show up so well in the rigours of competition. Duns either drew the pole position at the start or else
was very near the inside of the track, while I got the un-
welcome outside berth.

The start was bedlam. We had crowded together on th
line, each trying to edge as near the inside of the track a
possible. One boy went before the gun. The starter didn'
fire the recall, no doubt thinking life was too short for th
job of getting eight nervous schoolboys lined up agair
Arms, legs and bodies were jumbled in a wild kaleidoscope
Everybody wanted to get the inside position. I wanted t
get it, too, but there was a barrier of humanity in my way
For a moment I hesitated, not wishing to use brute forc
to lever a way through the mob. Then I saw Duns's re
head pulling away smartly from the ruck on my left. H
had got clear. Unless I got clear as well, this race might b
lost. Scruples were forgotten. I charged through th
human barrier to get across the track. My school-fellov
was in the way. I shouldered him rudely out of the way
Had he been sprawling at my feet I would cheerfully hav
trampled on him. So far as concerned me the hurly-burl
was over, though I believe it still went on behind. Duns wa
approaching the first of the left-hand, right-angled corner
I came up on him fast. The race was in hand. I knew i
I felt myself stronger than him. On the straight betwee
the two corners I would overtake him decisively and tha
would be the end of the affair. He skidded round the rigl
angle and I skidded after him, piling on the pressure
near enough to put out a hand and touch his shoulde:

I had actually drawn level with my opponent when
fell into an elephant trap. Or so it seemed. Rounding th
corner I had been vaguely aware of a discoloration of th
sacred turf ahead, but was too busy chasing after Duns t
consider what it might be. It turned out to be a long jum
pit filled with loose sand. What it was doing there, Go
knows. A narrow lane of turf, perhaps a yard wid
separated the side of the pit from the white line markin
the edge of the track. Duns ran on the turf. I, in the act

overtaking him, ran through the pit. It seemed a very long run. I didn't know what on earth had happened. The solid ground had been pulled from under my feet and I was being made to flounder through some sort of quagmire. Had I had sense, or experience, I would have spotted the danger, dropped back, and left my overtaking effort until later. But I was young. There was a chap in front of me. The sooner I got past him the better. Get out in front and stay there. That was the only rule of sprinting I knew. I tried to put it into practice on all occasions. This was a wrong occasion.

A clear five yards must have been lost through that obstacle left quite unforgivably in the path of a group of sprinters, a loss too big to be made good. My reward for the afternoon's work was a silver medal instead of a gold. But the defeat didn't trouble me, as did others in later years. For once I could attribute failure to bad luck. L. Duns hadn't beaten me, but Newcastle United's groundsman.

The boy, we know, fathers the man. That streak of ruthlessness needful if one is going to develop into an athlete of even average quality develops early, although at first it may not be recognised as ruthlessness. It may seem to be only one of the many ways in which the adolescent strives to assert himself as a person of consequence among his fellows. But it soon turns out to be something more than that. Mere boyish arrogance does not have this grim purpose about it. A dogged perseverance is not the most striking trait of character among the young, nor is fixity of intent. Where these traits are exhibited, they sweep aside more light-hearted and unpurposed opposition. We of our school did not simply want to beat other schools matched against us in athletics contests, we wanted to murder them. Other fellows might still regard running as a game. To us it was an article of religion. It wasn't our idea to be good losers, but good winners. The toil of training and the anxiety of competition were not endured just so that we could demonstrate nobility in defeat. Victory over self was our first object, and victory over others the second.

We had our times of levity, naturally, but these do not stay in the mind so much as the moments of strain and anxiety. When you go to the starting line for a hundred yards sprint, the world suddenly narrows. Not only does that strip of chalk-marked green turf or grey cinder come to have great importance, it seems to be the only thing that has existence. A bright light shines upon it, leaving the surroundings in a shadowy dimness. Your mind is concentrated, sharpened to a point. Already, in imagination, your body is arrowing down the track. You notice the little flags on the posts marking the start and the finish, seeing which way the breeze blows them, pleased if the current of air is going to be a help, disgruntled if it is going to hinder. You do a preliminary patter with your spiked shoes on turf or ash, that patter which is the sign of the true sprinter, the ability to strum your feet on the ground with something of the speed with which a stick vibrates on the tautened skin of a drum. The starter has blown his whistle. The judges and timekeepers at the finish have waved to show that they are ready. You take in deep breaths, sucking in oxygen. Your nerves shriek in protest against the idleness which they wish to see translated into violent action. The tension between you and the other runners can almost be seen, like the air which quivers up from overheated tarmacadam on a scorching summer's day. This is no game. This is no piece of frivolity for young fellows to amuse themselves with. At such a moment this is something more important than anything else in the world. You are putting body and spirit to a test in which you hope they will prove supreme.

Even to write those words brings on the familiar feeling. The heart begins to thump, the adrenalin flows, the lungs take in a great gulp of air, the nerves are naked and vibrant as they await that ringing call which has a message not only for the brain but for every fibre of the body – *'Get to your marks!'*

The rewards (if there be any) which result from this effort and striving are not valued for what they are intrinsically worth but for what they represent. The runner has a tendency to display only the finest, most hard-won scalps hanging from his belt and to forget about those taken from an inferior enemy. An easy victory brings no real satisfaction, but a narrowly-snatched win over a rival of equal calibre will lift the heart in exultation. The trophy recording that win will long be cherished.

Pot-hunters are often spoken of contemptuously, but it isn't the pots they see when they contemplate the row of more or less tarnished silver vessels on their sideboard, it is the achievements of which the pots are visible and tangible proof. The real pot-hunters (and they are few) are the runners who regard their pursuit as a means of collecting the practical trophies in the shape of personal or household goods offered as prizes at local handicap meetings, and as nothing more than that. But most runners aim beyond such humble foothills in the range of athletic endeavour, even if their aim should exceed their grasp. The true runner is a gold prospector. He wants to be a big frog, if only in a small puddle, and the mark of the big frog, or the champion, is the gold medal. In the nature of things champions are few at whatever level, but there are many dedicated to the search for this prime position. You can't make much use of gold medals except to embellish a watch chain or fashion a bracelet for your wife, but a hunger for them, once developed, isn't easily satisfied.

CHAPTER SEVEN

IN MANY RESPECTS a runner is like a pregnant woman. Both need to take suitable exercise: both will probably observe dietetic restrictions: both may feel the same anxiety over the state of the bowels: and both will be preoccupied with thoughts of a coming event. The runner's achievement, however, owes nothing to the intervention of a second party.

If the runner is a natural egoist, this egoism is constantly reinforced by the self-consideration required of him. He has to think about the state of fitness he has reached: about the further training necessary in order to reach peak fitness: about the series of competitions he must graduate through if he wants to progress towards a title race of some importance: about the tactics he should adopt in these races so as to defeat the opposition. Nearly all the runner's thought in regard to running is done from the viewpoint of self. It has to be. He is the particular sun of a little heliocentric universe.

If he were not a man already set apart by the nature of his pursuit, this self-centredness would make the runner so. He brings everything to the bar of his running for judgment. Habits, activities, interests that cannot prove a contribution to the great design get the axe. For fear of injury the runner will be wary of playing rough team games. He may well abjure the pleasures of wine and tobacco. Often he will pander to some fad in regard to his food or living habits. Even courting can come under the ban, because of its distracting effect upon the mind, if for no other reason. The runner takes care of himself, no doubt about it. A lot of people think he takes care of himself too much.

Most things connected with athletics originated in ancient Greece. So did the first criticism of the athlete's tendency to wrap himself in cotton wool. Plato made it. In the third book of the *Republic* he considers what sort of physical training would most benefit the citizens of his ideal state, and he comes down heavily in favour of military as opposed to athletic training. The soldier's exercises make him hardy and adaptable, Plato reckoned, mentally and physically equipped to suffer privation and to meet any kind of danger or emergency. The athlete's training is aimed at an exactly opposite end. He is pampered. He has to have special food. He exercises his body with only one limited objective in view. He is sheltered from any influence that might have an unfavourable effect upon his performance in competition. And that performance is of little value to the commonweal. Such a man is a useless drone, a burden on society. He, and others like him, must be excluded from the ideal state.

The athletes were in good company, for Plato proposed to shut out Homer as well, and not merely because the poet's heroes competed at running for cash prizes.

It sounds odd to speak in one breath of the runner undergoing a stern training programme and in the next of him coddling himself, yet the two statements are not incompatible. Runners who would go out to train in a blinding snowstorm avoid entering a cinema for fear of catching a cold. Men who intend to slog ten miles over really tough country will be as fussy about their pre-race light lunch as any fashion model with a mania for slimness.

Towards the end of my time at school I got a notion that a diet consisting mainly of wholemeal bread, butter, dates and water would set me humming like a dynamo on the track. God knows where the idea came from. It sounds now like the number one punishment diet meted out to ob-

93

streperous convicts in an Egyptian gaol. But for quite a while I lived on this meagre fare, and gladly. Apart from the physical benefit I hoped to get from the regimen there was also some mad notion of dedicating myself to my calling, some thought that I was marking myself off from those non-runners of coarser clay who poisoned their systems with roast beef and Yorkshire pudding.

Among the foreign merchants in the town where I lived was a Greek ship chandler called Dimitri. Actually, his name was Demetriou, but the Aliens Office had simplified it a little for their own convenience. Dimitri's shop was a dark, cavernous place, filled with the aroma of cinnamon bark and cloves and freshly-ground coffee. Greeks frequented it, and Maltese, and swarthy, hawk-nosed characters from the Levant, and dusky seamen who came out of latitudes within hailing distance of the Equator. It was a little enclave of the exotic in the prosaic surroundings of a north-east sea-port, but the presiding genius did not cut a very exotic figure. Dimitri came from Andros, in the Cyclades. A tall, heavy, square-faced man, he always dressed in a neat brown suit, black boots, and a bowler hat. Never in our acquaintance, whether in or out of doors, did I see him without the bowler hat. Mournfully, from underneath its brim, he looked out upon a world vastly different from that of his native island, lamenting his translation from blue skies and seas and honey-coloured rock and bone-soaking warmth to lead-grey clouds and east winds and rheumaticky damps.

'Holy Virgin,' he would say, standing in the doorway of his shop and watching the rain come down like a forest of steel rods, 'Holy Virgin, what a climate!'

But though he often talked of returning home, he never went.

It came out, in the course of the halting modern Greek

94

conversation which I practised with him, that I had ambitions as a runner.

'A runner!' he exclaimed. 'An athlete! By God, that is a fine thing to be!'

'No doubt, for anyone who becomes good at it.'

'But of course you will become good at it. By God, I was an athlete myself once, a discus-thrower. See, even now I have not forgotten the method.'

Reaching out he took hold of a circular barrel lid and then struck a pose behind the counter. It was a posture I have never seen a modern discus-thrower assume, though it bore some resemblance to that of Myron's Discobolos. Except that the Discobolos didn't wear a brown suit, nor have a black bowler hat stuck on his skull.

'By God, I could throw this thing for half a mile. Once, in the stadium at Athens, I actually hurled the discus out of the arena and broke a spectator's jaw.'

'Good heavens, he must have been very angry.'

'Angry? By God, he congratulated me on my throw!'

I said that sounded very forbearing of the spectator. Dimitri waved a hand impatiently.

'No true Greek would ever let personal discomfort interfere with his appreciation of a great athletic feat. Always we have been a people who loved contests of speed and strength. Always we have been great athletes. You know why?'

'No.'

'Because of oil.'

'Oil?'

'Of course. Olive oil.'

'You mean,' I felt I was some way behind him, 'you mean your athletes strengthen their limbs by massaging them with oil?'

'Massaging? By God, no. They strengthen their limbs by drinking it!' He flung his head back and opened his

95

mouth and went through the motions of one taking in a hogshead of oil. 'The oil saturates their whole body. It percolates into their muscles. It oozes out through the pores of their skin. By God, when they sweat, they do not sweat sweat, they sweat olive oil. Their limbs are always lubricated. The film of oil on the skin gives protection from the cold. Never are they unhealthy. We Greeks are the healthiest people in the world.' He turned his head away and a rich, bronchial cough interrupted his flow of words. 'Except, of course, in this diabolical climate.'

Ill-informed though I was about the body's working, it seemed to me unlikely that any liquid could pass from stomach to skin, as Dimitri said olive oil did, without suffering some sea change on the way. I ventured a mild scepticism.

'By God, I tell you truth!' Dimitri exclaimed. 'What gave Philippides such great strength in the olden times? How was it that Spiridion Louis won the first Marathon in the Olympic Games of modern times? Oil, I tell you, oil was the secret!'

About Philippides's diet I didn't think Dimitri would know any more than I did, if as much, but the confident statement about Spiridion Louis impressed me. Later I learnt that other people had other theories to account for Louis's success in the first Marathon – his drinking of a glass of wine halfway through the race, his knowledge of the rugged country between the Bridge of Marathon and the stadium at Athens, or simply, and most likely, the stamina he had built up by enduring many forced marches as a conscript soldier. However, Louis had won, and in 1896 Dimitri was of an age to have heard about the victor's training methods, so I listened to the oil theory, as I would have listened to anyone who spoke with conviction about running.

'But, by God, do not believe me without proof.' Dramatically Dimitri reached to a shelf behind him and brought down a large bottle of olive oil. 'Here, my friend, accept this. Take two tablespoonfuls every day before breakfast. Soon you will notice the difference. Your limbs will become more supple. Your skin will shine. Your digestion will improve. By God, you will become a great runner!'

The prophecy, alas, proved untrue, but I made trial of the olive oil prescription. I made trial of many other prescriptions. If someone had solemnly told me that hair shirts were being worn by all the best runners, and that they induced a startling turn of speed, I should have gone to get measured for one without delay. But I'd have found myself at the end of a long queue. There would have been many other customers for hair shirts.

Only three things make for success on the running track – physical ability: preparation: and mental keenness. Yet time and again runners, and not always the most ingenuous, will seek some elixir, some talisman, some philosopher's stone which will transmute the base metal of their mediocre capacity into the fine gold of championship class. In my youth there were runners, and I'm sure there still are, who looked upon certain brands of liniment and embrocation as having almost magical body-building properties. Other men hoped to acquire extra muscle power from the fingers of the masseur, oblivious of the fact that what makes a muscle strong is use. Physical culture had its adherents, chaps who devoted more thought to the enlargement of their biceps than a figure-conscious woman does to the development of her bust. Living in a seaside town the salt-water fanatics were not lacking, hardy characters who trudged knee-deep through the sea even in bitter weather, firm in the faith that the brine bath was toughening their calves and ankles.

We also had Bunghole.

97

Bunghole's theory was that athletic ability depended on inner cleanliness. His preoccupation with his alimentary canal was almost morbid. A keen student of laxative advertisements, he treasured a vividly-coloured diagram which portrayed the human internal organs from the top of the oesophagus to the fundament.

'Uneliminated waste products poison the system,' he would declare, presumably quoting from the text which had accompanied the diagram. 'And you can see the difficulty, can't you? All those yards and yards of pipe curled up inside you like a nest of bloody pythons. Blockages are bound to occur. You've got to take steps to clear away unwanted matter.'

We, who did not seem to experience Bunghole's difficulty over such clearance, nodded sympathetically. 'What steps are you taking this time, Bunghole?'

'I saw in the paper the other day about a new breakfast food. It's absolutely guaranteed to ease your system with gentle massage, and to bring that bloom of perfect health to the skin. I've just started taking it. By the time the Polytechnic Sports come round I should be in peak condition.'

The Polytechnic Sports came round. Whether Bunghole was in peak condition or not, he didn't manage to get through his heat of the men's 100 yards flat handicap. It didn't need an expert on the internal organs to tell the reason. The poor fellow was one of those who convince themselves they are sprinters when they have no more talent for sprinting than they have for deep-sea diving. He simply couldn't move his legs fast enough. In training, when he did a striding run at three-quarters speed, he looked quite impressive. Long legs moved with precision, head was correctly poised, arms drove with a neat, economical action. Only after watching him for a few moments did you suddenly realise that Bunghole wasn't doing his

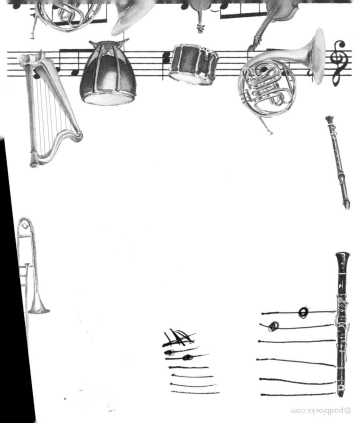

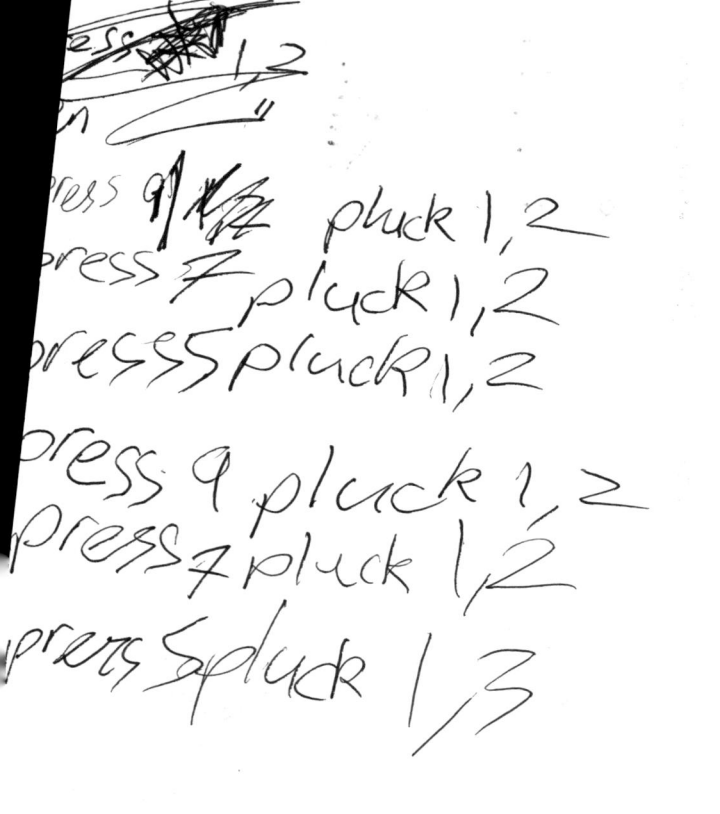

press ~~9~~ pluck 1, 2
press 7 pluck 1, 2
press 5 pluck 1, 2

press 9 pluck 1, 2
press 7 pluck 1, 2
press 5 pluck 1, 3

striding run at three-quarters speed, but at full speed. The motions were copybook, but they had no fire. He had never felt the true sprinter's urge. The only way you knew that he was taking part in a competitive sprint instead of in a training canter was when he screwed his face up into an agonised grimace.

But Bunghole's failure at the Polytechnic Sports didn't make him downcast.

'That damned patent breakfast food let me down,' he said. 'It's had no effect at all for the last few days. But I've got the answer now. A new aperient has just come out, a chemical, mark you, but none of your old harsh mineral salts. This stuff has a very mild, soothing action. It works while you sleep. The makers warrant it to be non-habit-forming. I calculate it should have me in good trim for the Cooperative meeting.'

Bunghole's calculations proved wrong again, if you can describe as calculations any working out of a proposition from such false premises. Although he was off 10 yards, he finished second last in his heat at the Cooperative meeting, an achievement only one degree less difficult than finishing last from such a mark. Bunghole looked very depressed afterwards.

'What's the matter?' I asked. 'The new stuff not working?'

He shook his head. 'It's working perfectly. That's what I can't understand.' His face clouded with unwonted doubt. 'You don't think – you don't think that the trouble is I can't run, do you?'

What can one say in reply to such a question? For all his obsession with his inside the man had at least tried to make himself a runner. He was conscientious in his training and he liked turning out at our local handicap meetings. These things were part of his life. In thinking he would ever make a sprinter he was deceiving himself, but the deception didn't hurt anyone, not even himself.

'Of course you can run,' I said. 'You've just had a spell of bad luck, that's all. Wait until the Infirmary meeting at Westoe. We shan't see you for dust.'

Bunghole looked wistfully at the case of silver teaspoons which was my reward for taking second place in the sprint handicap. 'Yes, they do you well at Westoe. The prizes are worth having. I'd like to pull off a place there. Maybe, if I changed to a different course of treatment. . . .'

We met early in the dressing tent at Westoe. The men's hundred yards wasn't due to start for another hour. Some wrestlers, Cumberland and Westmorland style, were going through their contortions out in the middle, but the meeting hadn't begun to warm up yet. Bunghole was the picture of despondency. He sat on a bench with his head between his hands. As I went over to him he looked up out of dark-shadowed eyes.

'That new course of treatment,' he lamented, 'it's an absolute wash-out. It hasn't even started working. I can feel the noxious substances poisoning my system and corroding my muscles. There isn't that clean, *swept* sensation inside. It's quite out of the question for me to run this afternoon.'

'But what is the new treatment?'

Bunghole displayed a flat tin box. 'A preparation that's just been put on the market. They're chocolate-coated tablets, very pleasant to the taste. Take one, and it's supposed to have instantaneous action. But I've already taken two this morning, without about as much effect as if I'd tried to move a concrete casemate. I tell you, I'm almost desperate!'

'Oh, come on, Bunghole, you can run a race even if you haven't done your daily dozen. Don't take what Napoleon said too seriously. Why not get changed, and do some warming up? Then you'll feel better.'

He shook his head. 'Impossible. How can a man run with all this refuse clogging his guts? I'm just a choked gutter.'

'But there's nearly an hour before the first heat of the men's hundred yards. Perhaps in your case these tablets won't have an instantaneous action, but a delayed one. There's still time for you to be an unchoked gutter before your heat comes on.'

Bunghole seemed a little less despondent. He looked at the flat tin box in his hand. 'Perhaps you're right. Yes, perhaps you're right. In fact, I'm not sure there isn't a faint qualm which indicates the log-jam may be breaking now. I'll make sure of it.' He tipped a couple of chocolate-coated tablets out on to his hand. 'These should give me a thorough scouring.'

Well, they were his guts, not mine. On any ordinary person the overdose would have had a catastrophic effect, but Bunghole's system was so used to ill-treatment that it took the punishment without a murmur.

Other runners were coming into the tent now, greetings were exchanged, clothes were flung on to the benches, a man stretched himself out on the massage table, the smell of liniment rose in the air, and the sound of flesh being slapped and pummelled. Going outside to limber up one could feel the interest of the crowd stirring as the meeting came to life. The red-faced, straining wrestlers had departed. Cyclists were doing practice laps of the grass track, or hurriedly changing flat-tyred wheels. Runners cantered up and down the hundred yards straight, high-stepping, or went through a brief programme of loosening exercises. The judges gathered at the finish, one of them unrolling a ball of worsted. The starter and his marksman walked towards their station near the handicap grid.

'Competitors for the first heat of the men's hundred yards,' the announcer's voice summoned through the amplifiers.

All of us taking part in the earlier rounds were pulled towards the start like iron filings clustering round a magnet. Bunghole and I were in heat 3. He seemed quite at ease, and nodded to me briskly as he jigged about. The running-off of heat 1 distracted me, but when the runners went forward to take their places on the grid for heat 2 I looked back in his direction. Now he did not seem to be quite so much at ease. He had ceased to jig around. A frown contracted his brows for a moment, and then cleared away. But the frown came back, followed by a spasm that contorted his features. The spasm also went, but the frown remained, the frown of a man occupied by a grave and serious thought. His jaw muscles tightened, perhaps a reflex action prompted by a restraint being exercised elsewhere upon the body. He moved a hand and pressed it against his midriff. All at once the expression on his face was tense, even hunted. He moved about in jerky little steps. In the evening sunshine I could see small dewdrops of sweat standing up on his brow. His teeth were clenched. A faint, despairing moan came through them. He held his whole body taut and rigid as a bow-string. The man was suffering agony. In front of several thousand people his gutter was threatening to unchoke. No worse moment could possibly have been chosen, when he was due to run in the next heat. Already the men in heat 2 were coming to the 'Get set!' position. The rigidity had gone out of Bunghole's body now. He writhed, like a snake with its back broken under the wheels of a car. The pistol fired.

It is the only time I have seen runners in a sprint race entirely ignored by the crowd. Instead of gazing at the men moving down the track, eyes were fixed on Bunghole moving at right angles away from the track. His summons could no longer be denied. With an obvious, clamant urgency he sped over the grass, his legs a pinky-white blur as they scissored, his arms pumping with the power of a desperate man. This was no three-quarter pace striding run but a tremendous, masterful sprint, the racing of a man who stood head and shoulders above the fellows competing on the hundred yards track. Bunghole was having his finest moment, at last proving himself as a runner. But the terminus of his great effort, instead of a line of worsted, was a wooden door.

As I grew up and moved round the dressing tents set up on cricket grounds and football pitches in the north-east, I imbibed sense and nonsense about running in roughly equal proportions. The sense did good, the nonsense did no great harm since, on being put to the test, it quickly proved its own worthlessness. The mere amount of myth and legend and ill-founded theory in circulation showed the extent to which runners, even of the humblest calibre, felt gripped by their pursuit. Being an affair of the heart and of the bowels as much as, or even more than, of the brain, it should cause no surprise if the devotee's view of running is not always strictly rational.

It isn't reason, it isn't a judicious balancing of advantage against disadvantage, which drives a man forward when he has long since passed the point of physical exhaustion. It wasn't a weighing of pros and cons in the Empire Games Marathon at Vancouver that spurred J. H. Peters on until he had got beyond the point where he could reason, until both his body and mind were utterly incapacitated, and only the blind will somewhere deep inside him dragged his unconscious self up from the track where it had fallen and made him progress over that ghastly final lap in a series of lurching steps and falls until, under the cruelty of it all, even the will surrendered. The 'reasonable' man on this occasion was the ultimate winner, J. McGhee, who, while

Peters was stumbling round the track on the final lap, had sat down by the roadside some distance from the stadium and was on the point of retiring. When he got word of Peters's disqualification McGhee pulled himself together and finished the race. It was a gallant effort and worthy victory on his part, but there can be no question whose was the greater glory.

Where men force Nature out of its normal mould, driving themselves to an intensity of effort which they alone can sustain with no moral or physical help from any other person or agency, they may subconsciously feel the need to compensate for the abnormality by clinging to some irrational belief or moral prop of their own imagining and construction. Bunghole's preoccupation with his meta-bolism, Dimitri's belief in the efficacy of olive oil, other men's passionate worship of the liniment bottle, these things were life-lines. Crazy? You may right. They wrote off Columbus as crazy, and doubtless he was in some respects, but he did discover America even if he happened to be looking for Japan. Agreed also that an obsession is a luxury which will have to be paid for in some way or other, but a runner, unlike Columbus, will rarely finish up in chains as a result of indulging in his obsession.

Not only runners have quirks and queer notions, but many other people associated with the world of athletics. My first pair of spiked shoes was made for me by a man who had a theory that a runner's footgear should fit as tightly as a pair of kid dress gloves would fit his hands. Somehow he managed not to see that the point about tight gloves, as about tight lacing, was that they had an elegant slimming effect upon the members they endued. This is not the main object of a pair of running shoes, though they should certainly grip the feet closely so that there is no danger of them coming off in the stress of competition. There was never any trouble about my first spikes coming off. The trouble was to get them on, and, when on, to endure the agony of their constriction. Later, when I was more experienced, I would have stood out against the shoe-maker's theory and thus saved myself the frequent pain of skinned and blistered toes, but I was young and the man pressed his case so confidently that I had no doubt of its truth.

Yet, considerable as was the discomfort I suffered through those shoes, the delight of moving in them (after I had forced the soft leather to the shape of my feet) was an enchantment. To sprint in rubber-soled gym shoes is a cumbersome and frustrating business. They grip a juicy grass surface, especially if the grass be wet, quite inadequately. Even on cinders or hard bare earth you can feel the slight slither as the forepart of the shoe refuses to lock with the point of contact as it comes under strain. The basic drive in sprinting comes from thrusting with the toes and the ball of the foot. Where the resistance they meet is not firm, there the thrust will not be efficient. Effort will be wasted.

Until I first ran in those long-spiked shoes I had not realised how much effort. Now there was no sign of skid, no danger of a slither which might throw you off balance or even make you stumble to the ground. The spikes bit crisply into the surface, made your drive rock-steady. Your confidence grew at once. You didn't have to impose any restraint on yourself for fear of a slip. You could run with the brakes right off. Your movement was faster partly because no effort was being wasted, partly because the exhilaration induced by that knowledge seemed to tap reservoirs of power previously unsuspected. Your feet seemed to fly, lightly and yet with power, as if you'd donned a pair of winged sandals.

Another stage had been passed on the road to becoming a runner. I mean, a real runner.

CHAPTER EIGHT

IN ATHLETIC COMPETITION the runner submits to two tests – the subjective test against the human opponents with whom he is pitted, and the objective test against the watch. Of these, the subjective test is by far the more important. The watch is impersonal. It has no feelings about you one way or the other. To a watch it is immaterial whether you run in a training sprint on a school playing field or in a national championship at the White City. It will record the same time in either case provided you run at the same speed over a given distance of ground.

But a human opponent is personal, immediate, hostile. He doesn't want to record you but to beat you. It is material to him either that you should not run your best or that his best should be better than yours. He, and others racing against you, will seek to establish a moral ascendancy. Their antagonism is not shown by the thrust of a sword or the sweep of an axe but by the invisible pressure of the will. Though they cannot be seen, your will and the will of an opponent lock in conflict as closely as the bodies of wrestlers. It is not only by reason of physical ability that a man emerges as victor from a race but because he has been able to assert himself mentally against a group of other men who were seeking to do him down.

Many men in training have promised to be first class runners, showing strength and speed and fire in their movements. The same men have been failures, if only comparative failures, in competition. This not because their ability was suddenly taken away from them but because their resolution wilted in the furnace heat of struggle. They could not stick out against the jostling, mental as well as physical. What may also worry such men is the knowledge that a training run can be repeated, but a competition run is for ever. The stakes are laid, the croupier has cried 'Les jeux sont faits,' the wheel is spun. What the man now does, he cannot afterwards undo. Before such stern finality determination sometimes falters.

Over a timed trial, in private, the conditions are in the runner's favour. There is no unfamiliarity of scene, no expectant crowd to unnerve him, no opponents who might make themselves awkward. Anyone present will be on his side, adding inclination to his inclination instead of subtracting from it. Should the trial begin and the runner not be quite satisfied with some aspect of it he can stop and begin all over again. But in a competition he can't stop. In a competition he can't pick his ground, ensure a favourable audience, or dictate the conditions of running – or if he does dictate them it will only be by asserting his own wishes against those of a number of other men. That is what stamps a man as a good competitor, the ability to show an aggressive spirit no matter what the place or the sympathies of the onlookers or the opposition.

In the world of athletics the supreme struggle is the prolonged, arduous and intensive competition of the Olympic Games. By those not very knowledgeable about running, a world's record may be considered the climactic achievement of a man's career. But an Olympic title is worth a hatful of world's records. You can set up a record when it suits you, when conditions are in your favour, in the company of pace-makers who are willing to play the role of Sherpa in your assault on Everest. In the Olympic Games you take conditions as they come and wherever they come, and you take them in the company of a large number of men who are anxious to be as unhelpful to you as possible.

Your contest is spread over several days. Certainly in the sprints, and perhaps in some of the shorter-distance races, you will have to fight your way to the final through a series of heats and quarter-finals and semi-finals. That is a process which sorts out the men from the boys. In no race can you reckon to coast home to victory, conserving strength for the subsequent races. You're trying the whole time, against first-rate opposition drawn from the nations of the world. The physical strain and mental anxiety are great. You must be able to endure, yet not let your dash and resilience be dulled by the endurance. As some rivals are eliminated, so does the quality of those who remain get even better. Only the cream of the cream survive to the final.

All the time the tension is increasing, as if someone were turning a screw. High drama presides over the arena where you compete, for these are the championships of the world that are being decided. The knowledge infects the crowd with an excitement that only an iron-willed runner could be proof against, and such runners are rare. No more than once in four years does a man get a chance to prove himself in such a contest. If he fails at this meeting the odds are very long against his succeeding at the next. Merely to reach the final against such an array of talent is just cause for pride. You're one of the six best in the world. But you're not content with that rating. You're out to prove yourself the best – and if you break the tape in your final there can be no arguing. You've proved yourself triumphantly as both runner and competitor. You join the band of victors which even after sixty years is still very small, still very select. You've reached a pinnacle from which you cannot be cast down. In the days of ancient Greece an Olympic winner was held in such honour that the year was named after him. That honour does not accrue to a modern victor, but he may well find that his gold medal brings material benefits in his later life.

Without an inner core of steel to your temperament you

cannot hope to win such a medal.

As a matter of athletics history, R. G. Bannister's running of the first mile in under four minutes in 1954 is noteworthy. He did something which many people said could not be done. But he did it with everything in his favour, except the weather. The crowd at the Iffley Road ground in Oxford were solidly on his side, lending moral support. He had pace-makers who worked for him efficiently and loyally. He had prepared himself meticulously for the attempt, and was spurred by the knowledge that others in the world were striving to achieve the same ambition. As a planned, almost clinically detached exercise the run was admirable, though this is not to belittle the part played in it by flesh and blood and brain.

But in the realm of competition running I would rate Bannister's victory later that year in the European Games 1500 metres as more meritorious. For between May and late August he had hoisted himself up as a target on which the finest middle-distance runners in the world had set their sights. Any doubts about his supremacy among milers had been resolved at Vancouver when he defeated his only serious Commonwealth rival, and the only other sub-four minute miler of the day, J. L. Landy. Bannister occupied a lonely eminence. Any one of a number of men would have been happy to drag him from it. He went to Berne as obvious favourite for the European 1500 metres title, and with Press and public almost hysterically interested in his performance. For several months he had had to remain in first-class physical shape and with a mind constantly honed to competition keenness. The strain must have been agonising. To be favourite for a title at a great athletics jamboree is worse than being an Aunt Sally, offering yourself to be shied at by all comers. When he went on to the track for his final Bannister knew that every one of eleven opponents regarded him as the chief opponent. Eleven men were out to get him, were out to prove their own merit by beating Bannister. And these were no contemptible enemies. Lueg, Jungwirth, Nielsen, Iharos, all were great names in middle distance running, all were resolute competitors. Bannister was no longer fighting against the watch in familiar surroundings with the help of friends. He found himself in a contest of giants where his reputation did not help and where only his strength and speed and determination would be of avail. That was when the man really showed his worth as a runner.

Exposure to competition can weaken confidence as surely as strong acid eats into metal. In the earlier, junior stages of running (once one has got over the shock which comes from doing anything in public) that fact is not appreciated. To the boy and youth the world is not such a hostile place, for he has only a limited view of it. Dragons are few. He competes in a small arena where enemies soon become known. If familiarity does not make them contemptible, at least they cease to frighten. Even the top trials, in the shape of county championships, are local affairs, held in a familiar setting and with familiar faces and voices present to give assurance that the fight is not taking place unaided. All this may lead to a false estimate of one's worth.

For the stay-at-home, that estimate will be based on the general standard of running in the district. A youth running at school or in junior club events in Surrey, a county rich in first-class athletes, will learn that he has to set his sights very high if he wishes to become a performer of any worth. In our district we had only two men of international status, J. A. Burns of Elswick Harriers and J. H. Potts of Saltwell Harriers. Both these men were long distance runners. In all other events, local standards were mediocre.

Sprinters and middle distance men were neither able to observe nor take part in high-grade competition on Tyne or Wear. A rare glimpse of men like Jack London wasn't enough to give the feel of top-class athletics. When we got away from our own stamping ground and entered for regional or national contests it was like jumping into the deep end of a pool when you have barely learnt to swim. Only we didn't realise that. We thought we could swim, pretty well.

In 1935, at eighteen, I took my own plunge. The main events in my calendar of running for that summer were to be the Northern Counties junior hundred yards at Ilkeston, the A.A.A. junior hundred yards and furlong at the White City, and the Northumberland and Durham senior hundred yards on my home ground at Westoe. (For junior county championships at that time eighteen years was the age limit, but for regional and national events the limit was nineteen. Thus one could be a man locally while remaining a boy nationally.) To undertake this programme it will be seen that some travelling was necessary. In this connection, a prospective runner would do well to live in the Home Counties, or, at farthest, in the Midlands. As the distance of dwelling from London increases, so do the cost and labour of taking part in competitions of any significance.

Ilkeston might have been Indian territory for all I knew of it. To get there took six hours in a coach, travelling with a party of Durham University athletes. I was off my own midden. In this Derbyshire town no one would know me, no one would give a damn about me. Any recognition I got on the broad, flat, beautifully smooth turf of the County cricket ground would be based not on past but on present performance. At first, I did not find the thought troubling. No qualms stirred during the long coach journey Three gold medals and a silver medal won in the two previous years seemed satisfactory proof of ability. The fact that this next demonstration of ability would take place in Derbyshire instead of in Sunderland or Newcastle was encouraging rather than the reverse. I had Spuggy's assurance that he would not have entered me for this sterner test had he not thought I could measure up to it. A fellow didn't want to stay in the junior league all his life. The point came when he had to step out towards wider horizons, move from the small puddle to the bigger puddle, and to yet bigger puddles after that. It was no more than a process of natural growth. What the term of that growth would be I couldn't say. It might already have come for others, it hadn't come for me. Everyone said so. 'Fain would I climb, but that I fear to fall,' was not in my book. As one progressed in sport, or in any other human activity, various tasks were set before one in an ascending order of difficulty. One performed these tasks, and with satisfactory results. Success seemed inevitable.

With an air of austere pride I showed my competitor's ticket at the gate, giving a condescending glance at the spectators who were ticking through the turnstile. They weren't runners. They had come to watch, not to do. I was one of the doers that they would watch.

At exactly what point the first dark flower of doubt began to blossom is uncertain. Perhaps the unfamiliarity of the scene had a delayed unnerving effect which hit me all the more sharply because of the delay. Or possibly I had found it easier to endure this sudden loneliness in thought than I did to bear it in fact. Or it may have been the sight of several young fellows running with power and urgency as they limbered up that caused the doubt to bud and unfold. I couldn't remember being so impressed by the speed of antagonists in my home territory. At home the antagonists had seemed slighter, less dashing, not so strong and determined. But this wasn't my home territory. This was enemy country. A vision of the wide area from which today's runners had been drawn suddenly unrolled in my mind. Manchester, Liverpool, Sheffield, Leeds, Bradford, all the cities and big towns of industrial Lancashire and Yorkshire with a lot of other counties thrown in – fellows had been combed out of these great centres to form today's opposition. And the fellows wouldn't be novices. In their own local puddles they would all be big frogs, as I reckoned I was in mine. All were seeking to move up to the puddle next in size. No doubt they viewed their own prospects no less rosily than I had done. Success against these would not be a foregone conclusion, as it had become in the north-east. Success here would have to be fought for.

The flower of doubt grew. A faint feeling of weakness assailed the knees. With quick anxiety I tried to convert what had been a feeling of unthinking confidence into a feeling of sober resolution. In the dressing tent young men were talking to each other and laughing. There was no one to talk and laugh with me, no one to inject spirit with a cheerful word. The attitude of the other fellows might suggest that they saw no great danger in this latest arrival. Was it possible they were right?

The sun shone brilliantly. Only the faintest zephyr stirred the warm and comforting air. A perfect day for sprinting, but I saw no perfection. The flower of doubt sprang up rapidly, choking me, blackening my mood. Resolution would not come in response to the urgent summons. Perhaps action would improve the state of mind. For a little while it did. Jogging in gym shoes round the quarter-mile track stirred up the blood, brought life back into the limbs, distracted the thoughts from the ordeal that lay ahead. But the distraction was not complete. The sight of spectators thickening on the benches renewed the doubt. They had come to watch doers. What if one of the doers proved to be an utter failure? My throat was dry. I felt scared.

The echoing reports as the starter tested his guns acted like water on salt, dissolving determination. The time of trial approached. Other competitors moved towards the hundred yards track. They looked keen, aggressive, assured. This was a long way to have come just to make a fool of myself.

'Competitors for heat 1!' an official shouted.

I was in heat 2. Only a few seconds separated me from the guillotine. First and second in each heat would go through to the final. The four also rans would pass into oblivion, not known because not worthy to be known. The runners in the first heat were getting down to their marks. I couldn't bear to look. My heart was pounding, but not in its natural place. It had broken adrift from its moorings. The rest of the body also seemed to be coming apart. My legs were as weak as columns of water. Black nausea rose in the guts. My God, this wasn't the 'needle', this was panic. The blood thundered in my head so that I hardly heard the gun. The first group of six had been despatched down the grass track. The six in heat 2 were now coming under starter's orders. I sat on the ground, trying to knot the leather laces of my spiked shoes. The last eyelet for one of the laces refused to let itself be found.

'Come along, there, number 10!' the marksman shouted impatiently.

It was done. I went up to the line. The only running I wished to do was in the direction of the dressing tent, but having put myself forward for a test, I had to go through with it. No time now to dig holes, without incurring the starter's further displeasure. I made do with the holes dug by the runner who had used the lane in the first heat. They didn't quite fit, but with the heavens crashing all around there seemed no point in complaining of a small discomfort. Too quickly for my liking the starter had us in the

Get set!' position. The preliminaries could have been protracted indefinitely for all I cared. But it seemed they were
already too protracted for some. One runner broke. The
rest of us eased ourselves out of our holes and took a few
loosening strides forward.

'Number 7!' the starter's marksman called, naming the
runner, warning him that if he broke again he would be dis-
qualified. The little incident gave me some comfort. So I
wasn't the only runner here in a sweat of apprehension.
Number 7 was apprehensive to the point where he thought
that a flying start would give him more chance of gaining
the desired first or second place. We got down again. Some of
the strength began to come back to my legs. The booming
in my head was not so thunderous. My heart pounded less
and seemed to have anchored itself back in the proper place
again.

Even so, my start was a poor one, more like the faltering
steps of a baby than the full-blooded drive of a sprinter
hurling himself into action. I could see others ahead of me.
A yard, perhaps two yards, had been lost at the gun. That
distance had to be got back, and quickly. Mists cleared from
the brain as if they had been swept away with a broom.
This was a time for action. Let thoughts and doubts go
hang. The grass track was crisp and firm and springy, invit-
ing movement. Almost without direction from the brain
the limbs began to reach and thrust with their familiar
power. I was doing well the thing that I knew I could do
well. The moment of trial at once showed what my ability
was in relation to that of the other runners. They may have
looked more aggressive at the start, they were less com-
petent on the track. Whether they came from Manchester
or Manchuria made no difference. I knew I could beat this
lot. By the half-way mark the distance lost at the start had
been made up. Doubt, anxiety, panic were all forgotten in

the delight which comes from the efficient performance of a chosen bodily exercise. I had been a fool to worry, but at least I had got over it. Let the others worry now. Let them fight out who was going to have second place. I had got the first place which ensured an appearance in the final. The six-hour journey in the coach had not been unnecessary.

In the event the coach journey brought the reward of a runner-up's silver medal. J. O. Jones, of Cheshire, beat me in the final by a couple of feet, returning the fair time for a junior of 10.4 seconds. The defeat caused no great disappointment. Jones was certainly good, and, it turned out, a junior runner of some reputation north of the Trent and Mersey. My own performance was quite the best I had done so far. It gave satisfaction to have measured up to this first challenge of a bigger puddle and, in so doing, to have overcome a personal weakness.

But an even bigger puddle lay ahead, and contemplation of it raised disturbing queries.

As well as a silver medal, two thoughts were taken away from Ilkeston. The first was a fuller appreciation of what lay in store at the White City in London in a fortnight's time. Ilkeston had been a regional affair, but the A.A.A. sprints were national championships. Runners from all England would be there, as well as youths from the other home countries and perhaps Continental countries as well. Dr Hahn's school at Salem regularly sent pupils across to take part in British sporting events. These were far horizons indeed. And the runners who came would be good. They weren't likely to make long and expensive journeys unless they had some hopes of success. Jones, my conqueror at Ilkeston, had been nominated by the Northern Counties A.A.A. as their official candidate for the White City hundred yards. That they hadn't nominated me was indication enough of what the N.C.A.A.A. thought of my prospects.

Earlier in the year reports had been made by one of our schoolmasters on the performance of A. Pennington in the Public Schools Sports. He had clocked 10.3 seconds for the hundred yards, and looked impressive in doing so. Already the *cognoscenti* of athletics were predicting a considerable future for Pennington. Perhaps he would be another contestant in the 3 A's. It looked like being a very tough field. Measuring myself against Jones, the only yardstick I had, I ought not to be completely at sea against such opposition, but the chances of putting up a noteworthy performance seemed on the small side.

They seemed even smaller when I pondered the second thought. For the first time, before that heat of the Northern Counties sprint, I had known bad stage fright, stage fright so severe as to be almost incapacitating. For the first time I realised how it was possible for a runner to defeat himself, merely by brooding about a competition before he actually took part in it. The realisation did not at once weigh heavily, since the thought was quite a new one and in any case I had overcome the stage fright. But could I be certain of overcoming it again, should it recur a second time? Perhaps so, but there was a vaguely uneasy feeling that a chink in one's mental armour, once disclosed, might re-open despite all efforts to patch it up. The mere fact of its being contemplated might make it re-open. Very well, then, do no contemplating. But that wasn't easy. One had reached a stage of self-consciousness. Invincible ignorance could have taken up a blasé attitude about such an eminent tournament as the 3 A's junior championships, but dawning knowledge could not. The mind was bound to dwell on the meeting, going through the endless and futile business of calculating chances, even though honest calculation showed the chances to be slender.

Yet was the business so futile? If the mind, slanted one

way, could generate physical weakness, could it not, slanted another way, generate power? Was it possible by taking thought to increase one's chances, make them less slender?

Dr Coué would have said so. People might call Dr Coué a crank, but that didn't mean his ideas ought to be dismissed without examination. Not that there was anything so original in the ideas. Authority for them, in fact, could be found in the New Testament. But Coué dusted them off and polished them up and re-shaped them in a form more suited to modern consumption. In health, Couéism taught, the mind is all. You can deliberately think yourself into good health, or for that matter, into bad health.

Nowadays, when there is so much talk of psychosomatic conditions, doubtless Coué is written off as a mere raw and blundering pioneer. How the experts regarded him in *' * middle nineteen-thirties I don't know. At the time all that concerned me was whether his theory could be applied to induce extra strength, when health was already present. By willing it sufficiently could a man induce power in his limbs, or at least prevent loss of power? Could the mind conquer its own disease of doubt? ˉet, to do so, wouldn't it have to be a special sort of mind in the first place, the sort of mind that would never be seriously troubled by doubt? Didn't it boil down to this, that the strong man was strong by reason of strength already in him? And didn't it follow that a man who showed weakness did so because he wasn't strong enough to prevent it? And never would be strong enough?

Once having started, the process of self-examination went on relentlessly, lasting for a fortnight. Sometimes the mind pronounced a favourable verdict on the situation, more often an unfavourable. The more numerous the examinations became, the more I understood that the analysis should never have been attempted in the first place, and the less able I was to stop it. The squirrel was on the spinning treadmill in its cage, and it couldn't get off. One thing was quite plain. Coué's theory had truth in it. I had thought myself into a condition of doubt and uncertainty about my running. Such a condition would never have arisen had I closed my mind firmly to the panic at Ilkeston. There are certain things that are best stuffed down into the mental dustbin and forgotten about, and never mind any later burrowings they may contrive into the psyche or the soma.

For various reasons, mainly financial, my father and I travelled to London in an overnight train which left at 11 p.m. and arrived at King's Cross at 6.30 a.m. on the morning of the A.A.A. junior championships. It would have been better to arrive the day before. The journey took an uncomfortably long time, and there was little chance of sleep during it. However, to a fit young fellow of eighteen these drawbacks did not greatly matter. The body had enough vitality to do without rest for a little while. What did matter was the mental restlessness, the alternating fits of hope and despondency. The programme had arrived some days previously, detailing the competitors in the sprints. My main interest lay in the hundred yards. A. Pennington, the Public Schools champion, was not to be an opponent. (I saw quite enough of him later on, when we were both University runners.) According to the newspapers, J. O. Jones, the Northern title-holder, and D. S. Higgins, of Chiswick, were favourites for the short sprint at the White City, either of them being thought capable of beating the current championship record of 10.3 seconds.

During the short naps I took as the train rattled through the night these two names wove patterns in my brain. There were awful visions of myself trailing at the rear of a heat, time and money having been wasted on a most unprofitable venture, while Jones and/or Higgins sprinted so far ahead that they were almost lost sight of in the distance.

Even worse (though I rarely 'broke') was the vision of myself perpetrating two false starts and being pulled out of the race with ignominy without even having the chance to contest it. All the follies, errors and accidents of which sprinters are capable I committed many times over on that train journey. I had got myself beaten in the afternoon's events before I went anywhere near the White City track.

There must have been outward signs of the inner state. Over breakfast Father eyed me casually, or so it seemed, and then looked back at his plate.

'Feeling tired?' he asked.

'A bit.'

'Windy?'

A pause, while I pronged a piece of bacon. 'Not more than usual. I expect I'll be all right by this afternoon.'

All right by this afternoon? What a hope. There were six hours left. In that time, if I kept on at my present rate I could worry myself into a nervous break-down.

'You know,' Father said, 'you don't want to think about this race, not until you get on to the track.'

'I quite agree,' I said sarcastically, 'to think about it is the last thing I want. But now that I am thinking about it how do I stop myself?'

'That is a difficulty, of course.'

And a difficulty I saw no way of getting round, short of taking a sleeping pill or a course of hypnosis. Father paid the bill and we went out into Oxford Street. It was a blazing July day. He looked round cheerfully.

'You know,' he said, 'other times when I've been in London I've never had the chance to do any of the ordinary tourist sight-seeing. Do you feel like walking round for an hour or two, looking at the Metropolis?'

'But don't you think it'll be a bit tiring in this weather?'

'Not at all. I'll see that you're fit and fresh by lunch-time.'

He would see that I was fit and fresh by lunch-time? He saw to it that I was exhausted. He had decided that the only way to stop the squirrel galloping round on the treadmill in its cage was to kill it with fatigue, with a risk that other things might get killed in the process. We went almost as far east as the Tower, and worked back westwards to Marble Arch. The light glared out of a sky of pale brass, and the heat bounced off roadways and pavements, hitting us with a sense of physical shock. Never had I known concrete and tarmacadam to be so hard and tiring underfoot. After an hour I'd had enough, but Father always pretended there was something else he wanted to see, just a little way farther on. Although I'd already become quieter and more relaxed, there was still plenty of time left before the first event, time for me to go broody and defeatist again. So, although I grumbled and sweated, he enticed me forward.

The process, I realised later, was a delicately balanced one. Father wished to get me to the point where my mind would be relaxed and unconcerned, and yet not to the point of actual physical collapse. The first point was reached, and the second perilously near being reached. When at last we stopped for a light lunch I'd forgotten all about the White City. I had become too engrossed with the soreness of my feet. He let me take a nap afterwards, and woke me up in time to go to Wood Lane. The afternoon's racing held no terrors now. There was even a danger that my view of it would be too lethargic and detached. Some degree of nervous tension in a runner is essential, but my mind was calm and equable. Certainly my muscles have never been so thoroughly limbered up for a race before or since.

In any major contest it is beneficial not to be favourite. The knowledge that he is expected to win may make a man too anxious. He feels that he's on a hiding to nothing. Trying to justify predictions, trying to assert his expected supremacy, he will tend to 'press' and strain, thus giving some unnoticed and more relaxed outsider the chance to sneak past him. If that happens the favourite will find it hard to pull back his rival. He has had a march stolen on him. The fact will increase his anxiety. The extra anxiety will make him tense up all the more, and the tenseness will make his running deteriorate.

I know now I wasn't the only one climbing out of the tunnel and trotting on to the red cinder track who had been or were still experiencing mental agitation that day. At a rough guess, all the other thirty-five sprinters in the hundred yards had had the jitters. Amazingly, this is a fact which the runner nearly always overlooks. Completely bound up with his own cares, he imagines all others to be carefree. If you can get to the stage where you set your own nervousness in the scales against the nervousness of your opponents and strike a balance between the two, then you've got a brain which will stand you in good stead for racing. Watch a group of horses being skittish as their riders try to get them lined up under the tapes. Runners at the starting line are in much the same emotional condition, only convention doesn't allow them to kick their heels or bite their neighbours.

The first and second in each heat of the hundred yards would go forward to the semi-finals, and the first three in each semi-final to the final. Chances of elimination in the first round were therefore higher than in the second. This was a matter to be watched. I had been drawn in the same heat as Higgins, one of the two favourites. Apart from being fair-haired and good-looking, he was much like me – somewhat above average in height, broad-shouldered and chunky in build. Objectively I regarded him and the others. The objectivity wasn't a good sign at all. There ought to be more champing at the bit, more metaphorical kicking of heels. Having spent the morning being purged of worry I now wished that the purgation hadn't been so completely successful. It was a day for sprinting, with the air hot and still. But in order to sprint well you had to want to sprint, you had to be anxious about sprinting. At that moment my attitude about sprinting was that I could take it or leave it.

Desperately I tried to inject myself with the 'needle'. But the 'needle' wouldn't come. Alongside me one chap was shivering and gulping nervously. I suppose he thought I was enviably cool. So I was, too damn cool. With all my internal organs in their proper place and functioning at their proper rate, I got down to my marks. I was on the White City track for the first time. I was a pilgrim who had arrived at Mecca. The biggest test of my running career so far faced me, and I might have been facing a row of cabbages.

My start was a slow one. Higgins got away well. So did two of the other fellows. After about fifty yards I had pulled up into third position, but there was still one man between me and a place in the semi-finals. Higgins I was willing to let go, but the other runner had to be dropped. He was going hard, too hard to pull back easily. Fright suddenly sparked in me. I had come a hell of a long way for this contest, and gone to a lot of trouble over it. If I didn't take care I was going to be out of it when it had barely started. Only thirty yards to go. My coolness and objectivity had gone. I was anxious for the race. I pulled the stops out. The other man was coming back. He had faded into a grey shadow, seen out of the corner of one eye. That meant we were probably running level. The fire was beginning to flame. Ten yards to go and the shadow had grown fainter, as the man dropped astern. The tape was right on top of us. Higgins had broken it. The shadow had gone, and with great relief I ran second past the post.

It was the other favourite, J. O. Jones, whom I met in my

semi-final. Mature-looking, with dark hair brushed back, Jones was of rather slighter build than Higgins, but nevertheless well-muscled and with a smooth, assured action.

We exchanged perfunctory greetings. Having beaten me at Ilkeston, Jones could see no good reason why he shouldn't beat me again at the White City. For the moment I had no objection. My immediate aim was to get into the final. The time hadn't yet come to push the throttle wide open. The organisers of the meeting had arranged that the three rounds of the hundred yards should be run off in less than an hour, with only ten minutes separating semi-finals from final. A hundred yards isn't far to run, but it can tire one quite surprisingly. What I had to do, therefore, was keep some steam in the boiler for the final and yet perform well enough to make sure of getting there. I ran second to Jones. He returned 10.3 seconds, equalling the existing record for the A.A.A. junior hundred yards. In the other semi-final, Higgins won, also in 10.3 seconds.

The situation was perfect for an outsider. So far, the contest had gone exactly as predicted by the experts. Both favourites had got through to the final. Each would regard the other as his greatest danger. Each would watch the other very carefully. The remaining finalists had all been beaten by one or both of the favourites and any threat from them had no doubt been discounted. The draw for positions favoured me. We were running the race on the side of the track opposite the main stand, where the high hurdles are normally held. I drew lane 1, the pole position, with the grass 'middle' on my right and all the other runners on my left. Higgins was in lane 4 and Jones in lane 5. This meant that the favourites' concentration on each other would be heightened by proximity, while an opponent over in the distance in lane 1 wouldn't receive their immediate attention. If the favourites could be 'jumped' they might not be able to respond quickly.

Excitement was now working in me like yeast. Gone were all lethargy and detachment. This was the supreme race in junior running. Coming second in both heat and semi-final had not taken undue toll of nervous energy. I was anxious for the start, desperate to go, knowing I had it in me to mount a climactic effort. When I first entered it the White City impressed me as a remote and lofty stranger. It had not become a friend exactly, but there was nothing about it to be afraid of. Despite the bigness of the puddle, I wasn't out of place in it. These terrifying athletes from Britain and France and Germany were beings of an order no different from mine. Previous doubts and anxieties now seemed ridiculous. Confidence burned like a flame. With the greatest care I dug my holes in the red ash, testing them and then making a little adjustment to the perpendicular back of the right hole. The others had stripped off and got ready before me, but I didn't hurry. Let them wait, and perhaps get jittery in the waiting.

'Get to your marks!' the starter called.

Slow and deliberate, taking deep breaths, I walked forward past my holes and then backed into them, settling my spikes carefully, feeling the pressure of the ash on my right knee, splaying out my finger-tips on the starting line, rocking once, twice in a kind of minute rehearsal of the vivid motion into which I would shortly explode.

'Get set!'

Back came up horizontally, body leaned forward, finger-tips whitened as they took some of the strain of the body-weight, eyes were fixed on the spot where my first right-footed stride would hit. The mind wasn't blank or wool-gathering but visualising over and over again the movements of the start, concentrating on them, seeing them unroll in imagination like a reel of film. The other five competitors on the line might not have been there.

I never remember hearing the gun. All I knew was that I'd come out of my holes like a sling-shot, straight and true and steady, and that I was alone. Absolutely alone. The chalk-laned track before me was empty. It was empty on my left. There should have been a group of striving figures running level with me, but there wasn't. Even when a man is a foot or two behind you, you can see him out of the corner of your eye without turning your head or making any effort to look. He appears as a faint grey shadow. But there was no shadow. Only emptiness. Perhaps Higgins and Jones had been watching each other. If so, by God, they were now watching me. The solitude was glorious, intoxicating. Never had my legs worked with such smooth power, quite unstrained and relaxed, and yet pouring out a flow of energy that raced away with my body. Fifty yards from the tape and I might still have been in a race by myself. Of the others there came sound but no vision. What had I gained on the start? A yard? Two yards? Whatever the gain, it was being held. Far from the initial burst of energy taking it out of me, I seemed to be running faster with every stride. The sense of acceleration may have been illusory, but it was inspiring. The track reeled off. The finishing post advanced. Already I knew it. The outsider was going to win. They couldn't catch me now. Any late effort they might be making had come too late. This race was mine. My heart swelled with triumph. My gaze concentrated on a point about ten yards beyond the line of worsted. When I went through the worsted I still hadn't seen anybody.

Jones finished second, a clear yard behind. They told me I'd returned 10.1 seconds. Only a tenth of a second away from evens!

I was a junior champion of England. I had set up a national record. My head struck against the skies.

126

CHAPTER NINE

THE 'NATURAL' MAN runs in pursuit of a dinner, or to avoid becoming a dinner. Whether pursuer or pursued, he may feel a certain urgency in performing the exercise, but the urgency is of a physical kind and purely temporary and will terminate with the success or failure of the project. If he becomes a dinner he cannot long reflect upon the fact. If he escapes the fate this once then he is not likely to carry forward a brooding memory of it until the next time the danger arises. Each situation is met as it comes, and dealt with as circumstances allow. The 'natural' man's memory of danger and power of reasoning about it are limited. It is the civilised man whose face becomes sicklied o'er with the pale cast of thought through dwelling on failure, or who grows elevated on the wine of success. For the 'natural' man, success or failure are isolated events to be considered with little thought of antecedents or consequences. Civilised man sees them in a broad context of experience, as part of a pattern of behaviour which will be affected by them for better or for worse.

Civilised man, alas, is conscious of self, and no one more so than the runner.

Attend enough sports meetings and sooner or later you'll hear the comment on some athlete or other – 'Runs just like a machine, doesn't he?'

Maybe he does, but he isn't one. Even an iron man of the track can suffer from a stomach disorder, or, what is more incapacitating, an emotional distress intruding from his private life.

The thought that he has a private life away from the track comes as a shock sometimes even to the runner. In the absorption of his pursuit he tends to forget that he is a man who must work in order to live, who enjoys or otherwise intimate family relationships, who is involved in various ways with the world around him. But every now and then some factor from that world thrusts itself demandingly and distractingly on his attention. When it does, it will have a more adverse effect on his running than lack of training or a pulled muscle.

Worry about money, fear of losing a job, an upset over a girl, dread of failure in an important examination, all these have from time to time been responsible for poor performances by a runner. There is certainly no reason why the runner should be any more free of the cares of civilised life than the non-runner, but perhaps a twinge of pity may be felt for the poor wretch when he lines up for a momentous race and, instead of being able to give his whole mind and will to the trial facing him, he is more concerned with trying to shake the black dog of depression from his shoulders. But probably the non-runner, instead of feeling pity, will suggest that the fool should give up his running in order to pay attention to the personal problem causing his depression.

This is the sensible approach. As must be clear by now, runners are not always very sensible people. They have something of the good trouper in them. The show must go on.

For a medley relay race held between north-eastern clubs, our local club had some difficulty in raising a team. These races are held over a mile, the first man running 880 yards, the next two 220 yards each, and the anchor man 440 yards. We could raise the half-miler and the two sprinters all right, but were short of a quarter-miler. After much searching the club secretary got hold of a man called Blackett who had just come home on holiday from the job he had with a radio firm in southern England. We knew his ability from the running he had done before he left the district. He had once got down to 50.5 seconds for the quarter, not a world-beating time by any means but quite respectable and certainly adequate to deal with the other men he would meet in the anchor stage of the relay.

Blackett wasn't very anxious to turn out in the event. He had other ideas about the way he wanted to spend his holiday. But the secretary pressed him hard, telling him that the club couldn't otherwise field a team, so at last he agreed.

On the night of the race, Blackett arrived late at the ground. The rest of us had already changed and done our warming-up when he came on to the track, still in his outdoor clothes. His face was pale, his expression weary. I thought I detected a red inflammation round his eyes.

'Look,' he said to the secretary, 'would you mind if I didn't turn out tonight?'

'Not turn out?' The secretary was aghast. 'Why the hell not?'

'I just – I just don't feel like running.'

'You don't feel like running? For God's sake. But we're relying on you. The race is due to start in five minutes' time.'

'I thought maybe you could get a substitute.'

'Get a substitute? Five minutes before the race? What sort of damn silly idea is that? You promised you would turn out for us.'

'Yes, I know, but——'

'Hell, man you can't let us down just like that. There's nothing the matter with you, is there?'

'No.'

'Then what's to stop you running? If you drop out, the club will have to withdraw its team.'

Blackett looked at the ground. 'All right,' he said. 'I'll run.'

He might as well not have done so. On the half-mile leg our man came in second by two or three yards. The club secretary took over for the first furlong and cut down the lead so that I took over on level terms with the runner of the club we most feared. He fumbled the baton and lost his concentration for a vital half-second or so, and I came up to Blackett with what should have been a winning lead of about four yards.

Blackett threw it away. Or that's what it looked like. When he took the baton he had the preoccupied air of a man whose thoughts are miles away from the running track. Instead of going off hard, so as to confirm the lead and blunt the aggression of the man chasing him, he broke into a listless, lifeless canter which would have been inappropriate at the start of a six miles race. Within twenty yards the man behind had overtaken him decisively, and the anchor men of the other two teams were also coming up fast.

'Get going, Blackett!' our club secretary shouted. 'Wake up, man!'

Blackett woke up, literally, it seemed. The surge-past of the other runner made him aware of his surroundings, and of the task in hand. He tried to open out. You could see him trying. Tenseness came into his face and limbs. His pace improved, but not enough. The man in front still gained, only a little, but he still gained. Blackett fought with the track, fought with himself. To no avail. Instead of being four yards up he was four yards down. Far from getting those four yards back he was having to concede even more. He ran like a tired man, a man making an effort but whose heart wasn't in the effort. The secretary had come up beside me. He groaned.

'What a waste. What a bloody waste. That race was in the bag.'

We didn't win the relay. We didn't even come second. In the last few yards Blackett was overtaken again, when he had slowed almost to stopping point.

In a lowering silence we waited while he came up to us.

'I'm sorry, chaps,' he said. 'I'm afraid I let you down a bit.'

'Please don't mention it,' the secretary said.

'I did warn you I didn't feel like running tonight.'

'We got the idea eventually.'

'Please.' Blackett looked distressful. 'I really am sorry, but I did try all I knew.'

'You tried all you knew?' the secretary said. 'In that case you don't know enough. You ought to try running at a funeral next.'

'That's not very funny.'

'Huh?' We looked more closely at the pale, unhappy face. 'How do you mean?'

'My brother's being buried on Thursday. He got killed in an accident last night.'

At the time of the A.A.A. junior hundred yards thoughts that running could be affected by the world outside running had not occurred. Even the lesson of how mind could react on body was not well learnt. The stage fright at Ilkeston was forgotten, or perhaps not so much forgotten as glossed over, written off as an isolated lapse unlikely to happen again. A few days after the affair at the White City came the first test in senior running, the Northumberland and Durham men's hundred yards. Not a test of the most severe, it is true, for at the time good sprinters were by no means thick on the ground in the two north-eastern counties. Nevertheless it would serve to show whether the White City performance had been merely a freak.

As well as running ability, it would also test nerves. The race took place on my home ground, and I had the undesirable distinction of being favourite. If I won, people would say, 'Well, it's only what we expected.' If I lost, people would say, 'Well, I can't see what they're making so much fuss about that feller for.' My chief opponents in the sprint had been engaged in senior running for some time, and would certainly be out to show me that men's running was no easy row to hoe. Before the start of the race the announcer drew public attention to No. 5 and detailed his recent exploits in the heart of empire. The praise was gratifying – no runner, however modest, objects to a measure of public acclaim – but put its object even further out on a limb. No. 5 had been billed as an attraction. No. 5 was, in effect, being forecast as a likely winner. No. 5 was a reason why this crowd had paid money to attend the meeting. No. 5 had better give value for that money.

The publicity had no unnerving effect. The 'needle' was there, that sense of excitement which comes from nervous energy building up ready for the moment when violent action will be demanded of the body, but otherwise the race was taken on its merits. I won in 10.3 seconds. A few weeks previously I would have regarded such a time as a great achievement. Now it seemed mediocre, but I excused it on the grounds that the grass track wasn't notably fast and that I ran the last few yards with a pulled muscle in the right thigh. Still, I had made a rapid and successful transition from junior to senior running.

The transition was endorsed a few days later when the A.A.A. sent me a letter to say that I was regarded as a possible choice for the British team to take part in the

Olympic Games to be held in Berlin the following year.

This letter meant very little. Scores of runners must have received the same notice. It merely signified that the A.A.A. had drawn up a preliminary list of men from whom they thought their choice of a team might eventually be made, and that an eye would be kept on these men to see how they showed up during the competition season of 1936. Without further proof of worth there would be no selection. In the meantime, we'll be looking out for you. That's what the letter meant.

But to a young and unknown sprinter in the outback of England the letter testified that he had arrived on the scene. His accomplishment had received official recognition. The A.A.A. senior hundred yards of that year was won by A. W. Sweeney, of the R.A.F. and Milocarian, in 10.2 seconds, point one of a second slower than my winning time in the junior hundred. That was something at which to raise the eyebrows, something to underline the significance of the letter from the A.A.A. It is unrealistic to compare two races unless they share a common factor. So, then, I was un-realistic. Sweeney had done 10.2, I had done 10.1. These were recorded facts. You couldn't get away from them, nor from the obvious inference. Within two months a jump had been made from obscurity to a position of some reputation. A further jump should be within the competence of an ambitious young frog. That the further jump might com-prise representation of one's country at the Olympic Games suddenly seemed quite reasonable.

Looking back, the optimism still seems justified so long as one assumed that progress would continue at roughly the same rate. At the start of the 1935 season, 10.6 had seemed a good time for the hundred. By the end of it, half a second had been lopped off. To lop off another half-second would be too much to hope for, but the magic figure of 'level time' should now be within one's compass, and after that, entry into the much more select band of those who had recorded single figures. Nearly a whole year was available in which to improve performance. In the autumn I would go up to Cambridge, with its first-class University track, flourishing athletics club, coach, and all possible facilities. Surely if one could win the junior national championship from a school playing field, the senior championship should not be out of reach with the help of Fenner's?

Hopes were high. The world seemed a very agreeable place. A rosy glow hung over the future. No doubt some degree of complacency crept in. It would have been better to view the coming year as one prolonged challenge, in which improvement and recognition would constantly have to be fought for, instead of assuming that improvement would come as part of the natural order of things.

Ignorance can be a source of strength. Knowledge is a source of strength. The unhappy transition period between ignorance and knowledge rarely fails to be a source of weakness. A man setting out to climb a mountain, with no idea that he is involved in anything more than an enjoyable scramble and never dreaming of doubting his capacity, will probably go ahead and climb the mountain. But tell the man beforehand that this is a great peak he is attempting, that many notable climbers have only scaled it with the greatest difficulty or haven't even managed to scale it at all; ask him who the deuce he thinks he is to approach so blithely a task which many better men than him have flunked, and his attitude towards the climb will be much changed.

P. G. Wodehouse, in one of his stories, wrote of a middle-aged businessman who took up golf. He had no previous experience of the game but saw no reason why he shouldn't be as successful in playing it as he had been in his comnercial operations. He said as much to the other men in the club he had just joined. The other men frowned at the new member's ignorant confidence, and smiled at the rude shock it would soon receive. But there was no shock. The businessman took lessons from the professional in which he was told to keep his head down, his eye on the ball, his stance firm but not rigid, his swing controlled, and so on. Having received the instructions, he obeyed them implicitly. At once he began to strike the ball as if he were a scratch player of long experience, instead of a rank beginner. He simply did not realise that what he was doing was difficult. Only after the thought of its difficulty had been assiduously sown in his mind by his now grieved and jealous fellow club-members did he begin to top the ball or slice it or hook it or make air shots or commit the other follies proper to a tiro. It would have been better for the man's morale had he started off that way from the very first, without briefly tasting the glory which as a rule only comes to players who have established their worth over a long period of striving. His sense of inadequacy would have been less.

Shortly after going up to Cambridge I felt in much the same state of mind as Wodehouse's character. Until then I had worked hard and with resolution at my running, but in a kind of mental isolation, with little knowledge of the general context of the sport. The north-east was a long way from London, a long way even from Manchester and Birmingham, the big provincial centres of English running. Except in the long distances, where one had the examples of J. A. Burns and J. H. Potts to follow, standards on the track were no more than middling. One hadn't had to fight hard enough for recognition. There was no general plateau of accomplishment in the district against which to set one's own ability. The paucity of good sprinters, and the complete absence of men who had received international honours, meant that a youth growing up had no chance of moving in the company of the great, or even on the fringe of it. A youth moving in or near such company retains his respect for the big names, but sheds some of the awe with which he at first regarded them. Giants become men. The remote events in which they engage – regional and national championships, or international matches – become less remote. The youth grows up gradually into an awareness of the higher levels of running instead of having awareness thrust into his lap like a time bomb.

On me, Fenner's had something of a time bomb effect.

It was a beautiful ground, it was an old ground, it had seen a lot of men come and a lot of men go. Deeds of note had been done here, by runners who were no less notable. On this elm-shaded enclosure, with its unorthodox 600 yards track on which we ran right-hand inside, had performed giants of the distant and not so distant past, such men as G. M. Butler, H. M. Abrahams, D. G. A. Lowe, Lord Burghley and R. M. N. Tisdall, all of them Olympic medallists, and four of them victors. Some of the giants still interested themselves in University running, and we met them on athletics or social occasions. A. G. K. Brown, the finest quarter-miler Britain had produced to date (though Scots favouring E. H. Liddell might dispute the point) was in his second year. He was also a fine sprinter, and ran the hundred yards in 9.7 seconds on the Fenner's track, a time not allowed for record purposes since the straight dropped some 10 inches over its length.

The main reason for the existence of the Cambridge club and track was to compete against Oxford, a place in Oxfordshire, which also had its quota of Olympic heroes in the persons of B. G. D' U. Rudd, A. N. S. Jackson and A. I

Porritt. J. E. Lovelock, who at that time held much the same place in popular esteem as R. G. Bannister held recently, had not long gone down.

Both Fenner's and Iffley Road were thick with memories, thick with shadows, thick with greatness. The giants, observed at close quarters, remained obstinately tall. One freshman, at least, was over-awed by them. One freshman asked himself who the dickens he thought he was to thrust himself so brashly into such distinguished company.

Humility is a fine quality, but too big a dose of it is very lowering to the spirits. It makes one feel inadequate, whereupon one will be inadequate. In my first term at Fenner's I ran not poorly, but without the dash and fire that I had shown during the summer, and on which such high hopes had been built. The contrast was marked and worrying, and the worrying did nothing to improve matters.

Without the previous high hopes the inadequacy might not have mattered greatly. It could have acted as a spur towards its own overcoming. But earlier achievements were on record. They could be compared with present performance. Present performance wasn't measuring up to them. Nor was present performance worthy of the letter from the A.A.A. This looked like failure. The thought corroded the spirit and deadened the limbs. A factor helping to deepen the gloom was that A. Pennington, the Public Schools champion of 1935, had gone up to Oxford with much the same expectations based on his junior running as had been based on mine. Only he was living up to them. We met over the hundred in the Freshmen's Sports at Fenner's, and in the Varsity Sports at the White City. Each time he won quite confidently. With his long, reaching stride and his slight roll of the body, Pennington ran authoritatively, like a man who thinks he's going to win. Against him I ran like a man who fears he's going to lose.

137

In 1935 the A.A.A. had an eye on both him and me as prospects for Berlin. Deservedly, he went. Deservedly, I didn't.

But the failures of 1936 were not so gross as to run quite counter to all previous form, or to make me think that the goal I pursued was a chimera. There is a kind of ladder of athletics progress at Oxford and Cambridge which the freshman is expected to climb – selection for the Freshmen's Sports, selection for the Relay Races, membership of the Achilles Club, selection for the Varsity Sports themselves. The ladder was duly climbed, and without delays. But whereas Pennington, in climbing his ladder at Oxford, ran up to his previous promise, I ran below mine. He competed in the 1936 Varsity Sports as Oxford's first string in the hundred, with a full Blue. I ran as second string to M. M. Scarr, and got a half-Blue. With Berlin only four months away, that difference seemed ominous.

Naturally the year was far from one of unrelieved gloom. In April there came a pleasant outing to France to take part in the $15\frac{1}{2}$ miles relay race through the streets of Paris for the trophy donated by the newspaper *Le Jour*. Each team had fifty runners, our U.A.U. task force being drawn from different Universities of England and Wales. We approached the contest in a more light-hearted spirit than some of the Continental teams. Several of our men only left the haunts of pleasure in the morning in time to board the coaches which took us to the different change-over stations, but we won the trophy.

Occasions such as these, plus selection for the annual affray against Oxford at the White City, might have added up to a satisfactory total for one who had gone up to Cambridge with the intention of making his way gradually in University running. That hadn't been my intention. Marked improvement on my running of the previous year, marked enough to catch the attention of the Olympic Games selectors, was what I sought. That improvement didn't come. The best time I did over the hundred in 1936 was 10.2. This had been the year when I was to get down to evens first, and then break into single figures. Instead, I couldn't even repeat the time recorded in the 3 A's junior hundred.

By now it was obvious to the reason that I had no hope of going to Berlin except as a spectator. The bus, which ran only once every four years, had been missed. In that summer's Northumberland and Durham sprint championship I ran second. Reason nodded its head sadly at this further confirmation of the recession from the standards of the previous year. But dreams and wishes made their voice heard above the call of reason. The bus was moving away, but it might still be caught. A good performance in the A.A.A. championships could still earn a place in the British team. On the basis of running earlier in the season a good performance was most unlikely. Never mind. A year ago I had gone to the White City in July not expecting any startling success, and had confounded both experts and myself. Why shouldn't the same thing happen again? At least if I reached the final of the 100 yards I would have saved something from the wreck of this year, I would have saved my self-respect.

Suddenly it became desperately important to get into that final. The internecine strife between Oxford and Cambridge was an engrossing business, but it shouldn't engross one too far. National recognition as a runner would only be accorded to a man who did well in a national event. With the prospect of a ticket to Berlin as the reward, the 1936 championships would be hard fought. Men from Holland, Poland and Australia were going to compete alongside native athletes. To reach the final against such opposition would not simply be a salving of self-respect. It would be quite a feat in itself. Here was a thread of hope. Grab it with both hands!

But through excessive brooding on mere part-success, the nerve had failed. The prospect of the contest did not induce a feeling of excitement so much as a feeling of dread. Even the most wishful thinking could not convince that this last chance was more than the slenderest. The finality of the affair turned the bowels to liquid. There was no spearhead of resolution, sharp and shining, but only a dull obstinacy. A year ago the White City had been warm and bright in the sunshine. This time it was grey and chill. Influenced by the weather, the blood ran even cooler than before. Instead of creating confidence, memories of the other, triumphant occasion merely deepened the sense of inadequacy. Heats, semi-finals and final were to be run in the hundred yards. Except for C. A. Wiard, of Blackheath Harriers, there was no one especially notable in my heat. To gain a second place in the heat and thus move up into a semi-final ought to be possible.

Apathetically I dug my holes. The other runners were jigging around, taking deep breaths, high-stepping, obviously keyed up at the prospect of the race. Beside them I felt heavy and lackadaisical. When we got down to our marks, my mind wouldn't concentrate. It wandered, thinking of Berlin, thinking of the season's mediocre efforts, thinking of how the promise had not been fulfilled. The gun took me by surprise. I was last away in a vital race when I should have been desperate to get first away. If my body hadn't reacted instinctively to the familiar stimulus of competition I should have been last at the finish. As it was, I came no better than fourth in a heat won in 10.2 seconds. Running as I had done a year ago I should have been through to the semi-finals. Now I was a mere also ran, forgotten, with no further part to play in the proceedings, indeed with no further interest in them. The guillotine had fallen. Once in this stadium my head had struck against the skies. Now it was rolling in the dust.

I thought I had reached the nadir.

I was quite wrong. The nadir was a good deal lower yet.

In the two seasons of 1936 and 1937 I didn't win a single race of any significance either at Fenner's or elsewhere. During the second season I didn't deserve to win one. Confidence, previously weakened, was finally broken by the debacle at the A.A.A. championships. A pulled muscle or other leg injury can be repaired by rest and treatment. Fitting together the pieces of shattered confidence is a more difficult matter. One becomes a zombie, going through motions mechanically without any spirit moving the limbs. I returned to Fenner's for my second year a man prepared to be beaten before he ever started a race.

The attitude of a freshman who had just come up was in marked contrast. In the A.A.A. junior championships of that summer H. E. Askew had run second in both sprint and furlong. Later he turned to long jumping, in which he had a long and honourable career, but when I first met him sprinting was his main interest. Askew, unlike myself at a similar stage, approached Fenner's with a brisk, business-like outlook. Seeking to win a Blue, he informed himself who the obstacles were to his attaining that ambition. They proved to be M. M. Scarr and myself. Later, he told me of the decision he took at the time. 'First I'll get Loader, and then I'll get Scarr. Brown I shan't worry about just yet.'

It is a good policy for a runner to follow, to get a 'hate' on those runners who are next above him in order of merit, to regard them as rungs on the ladder of his ambition, and then tread on them. Askew realised that A. G. K. Brown, who had come back from Berlin with the silver medal gained in the final of the Olympic 400 metres, was not suitable competition for him to cut his teeth on in senior running. Scarr and I were suitable. He went after us with determination. From me, he only got enough opposition to make the contest interesting. Had I not later got back at Askew decisively, and helped to turn his thoughts away from sprinting to long jumping, the story would hardly bear telling. The descent of Avernus had been so hideously easy. The fellow with the aggressive spirit, full of 'attack', gained the day over the man who had lost faith in himself.

Our main running at Fenner's in preparation for the annual joust against Oxford was done in the Michaelmas and Lent terms, when the weather is hardly at its best for outdoor athletics. Even so, it is difficult to believe that it could have been so consistently dark and gloomy as it appears in the memory. Much of the gloom must have derived from the state of mind. Training had become an irksome and monotonous chore. The bare branches of the elms sighed mournfully over the cinder circuit of funereal black. Sport had no taste in it, no savour. Legs felt weary long before an afternoon's training stint was over, and not with the weariness of work well done. Competition was approached reluctantly, and with forebodings. That hundred yards strip had become a house of little ease. Dully and doggedly one set about digging holes and doing a practice start, with a faint scintilla of hope that this time there might be some fire in the running. But it seemed that the fire was out for good.

Desperately trying to convince oneself that the trouble might lie in some fault of technique, studied attempts were made to run straight and smooth and with an almost geometrical precision. But the precision was an artificial thing. You might run direct and steady, your spike marks evenly spaced on the cinders in two lines that could almost have been drawn with a straight-edge. Other fellows simply ran faster.

So often you saw them pulling away from you, moving with relaxed ease while you strained despairingly, tensing your body and arms, feeling your legs going rigid from the effort. The more you tensed and strained, the worse your condition became. Your mind longed to be out there, in front, but some barrier stood in your way. Your feet were weighted down. This wasn't insubstantial air you were driving through, but some more solid, hostile obstacle. Hours, rather than seconds seemed to have elapsed since the firing of the gun. Defeat stared at you again, sombrely. No last-gasp spurt could save you now. In any case, such a spurt didn't come. You passed the winning post when the tape had already been broken by someone else. You felt a fatigue quite disproportionate to the amount of effort normally required over the short sprint. Your heart pounded and your head ached. You went over to pick up your track suit with all the sprightliness of a doddering ancient.

The condition was staleness, but not in the old sense of having over-taxed one's body with physical preparation. In the modern, and correct, view staleness is a mental condition. The body of a fit young man is capable of physical effort protracted almost indefinitely. It is his mind which revolts from work which it finds boring, tedious or fruitless. Repeated failure has a depressive effect. Even more depressive is the brooding on the failure, the feeling that no matter how much one tries, this burden cannot be shaken from the shoulders.

The best cure for the condition would have been to get right away from running for a while, to forget about it completely. In practice, this wasn't immediately possible. Joining a club, one undertakes certain responsibilities. Also, having run for the University against Oxford the previous year, it would have been a double line drawn across the ledger not to gain the same honour this year. The weary routine was endured, therefore, and the endurance got some reward when I ran as second string in the hundred to A. G. K. Brown in the 1937 Varsity Sports.

The really nagging, griping thought in this long period of failure was the fear that failure might be inevitable. Perhaps the promise shown in the summer of 1935 had been deceptive. It happens often enough that the transition from adolescence to early adulthood is marked by an efflorescence of vitality. This may find vent in displays of undergraduate high spirits, or in a carefree wielding of the cosh or chopper. Some young men suddenly flower as poets, or wits, or speakers at the Union; others become unexpectedly impressive on the sports field. Their vitality soars up rocket-like, making a great blaze and giving off many sparks, and then in a moment it is quenched. The promising young man is no more heard of. A gulf separates the showy qualities of youth from the more solid and enduring abilities of manhood. Trying to cross that gulf, many young men fall into it. It seemed that here was another one going to the bottom.

CHAPTER TEN

OUT OF TWO YEARS of comparative failure, one consolation at least emerges – the fact of not having given up. If tolerated long enough, despondency breeds its own cure. Descend into an abyss, and you eventually reach a point where further descent is impossible. After that, progress must be upwards.

Probably the upward turn is taken in spirit before it becomes realised and confirmed in fact. But fact strengthens growing inner conviction, and thereafter deed and conviction work together in a common task of reconstruction. If defeat generates defeatism which leads to further defeat, success also follows the same logic. The point is often made in more succinct, gnomic form, but gnomic sayings tend to lose their impact when they are repeated without being related to particular cases. You have to know all the frustration and unhappiness which lie behind the saying before you can fully appreciate its truth. You don't really know what the mill is until you've been through it.

The relay races held each year between Oxford and Cambridge were a less solemn affair than the full track and field meeting staged at the White City. They gave a chance to men who weren't likely to win a Blue to have some share in inter-University competition. Taking place either on the Iffley Road or the Fenner's track they were watched by partisan spectators who injected enthusiasm into the proceedings by the alternation of cheers or groans as their own team did well or ill. All the excitement of a local Derby was there, and the excitement usually found fuel to feed on.

Relay racing is the one form of competition where the runner is not out for himself but for his team. This often gives an extra drive and urgency to men who are normally mediocre performers.

Previously I had run in the relays as a member of the 4 x 110 yards and 4 x 220 yards teams. At the beginning of my third year at Cambridge I was also included in the 4 x 440 yards team. Never before having run a quarter-mile in competition, I had no idea how to set about the job. The distance was unexplored territory. For that reason it gave less cause for concern than the familiar distances. Every possible effort would be put into it, but if the effort failed there could be no great cause for self-reproach on the part of a man who did not pretend to be a specialist in the event.

The race, in fact, was approached with an untroubled mind, most refreshing after the doldrums of the previous year. Some said (and this was received doctrine at the time, though it is so no longer) that a quarter-mile should be run at a steady pace throughout, the idea being that the runner shouldn't exhaust himself over the first furlong and thus get into a state where he finished the second furlong on his hands and knees. This might be all right for a specialist quarter-miler, but how did a non-specialist know what the correct pace was in the first instance? Might it not be better for the non-specialist to go off almost as briskly as if he were setting out upon a single furlong, and, when that was finished, hope that he had enough strength left to carry on over the second furlong? That way at least he would know that he had put forth his maximum effort, whereas if he bothered himself with calculations of pace and distance he might well make some serious error.

Conscious that no one expected much of me, conscious that I didn't expect much of myself, I waited on the far side of Fenner's opposite the pavilion, while the first two legs of this relay were run. A. Pennington, who had now established himself not only as a sprinter but also as a quarter-miler capable of breaking forty-nine seconds, was to run the anchor stage for Oxford. R. A. Palmer would oppose him for Cambridge. Palmer, although a good natural runner, wasn't yet up to Pennington's standard. If he were to stave off the Oxford man's challenge it was essential that I should hand over to him with a good lead at the end of my leg. To achieve this I would prefer to start off with a good lead myself.

On a normal quarter-mile track all the take-overs in such a relay would have been carried out over the same zone, but on the Fenner's circuit of 600 yards they were at different points. Men accustomed to the standard oval were often confused and had their judgment upset by this odd arena. For someone to whom the quarter-mile was foreign it would have mattered little had the race been run in a straight line.

My opponent over the third leg was called Rideout. As the two men running the first stage passed us, we saw that the Cambridge man had established a short lead. This lead wasn't lost at the change-over, as so often happens. Our second runner maintained it for well over half of his distance. Excitement built up as we watched him and his rival striding down the home straight and then turning into the long curve past the pavilion. The spectators were shouting now, Cambridge voices being the ones mainly audible, urging on the home contestant. The waves of sound had a physical impact, making the flesh creep, accelerating the heart-beats. One was anxious to get on with the ordeal, and yet not get on with it. They were passing the third take-over zone now, where Pennington and Palmer waited. Hell, the Oxford man was suddenly pulling up. Our runner was tired. His head had started to go back. He was less than forty yards from the end of his stint, but he couldn't hold off his rival. The shouting crescendoed, Oxford voices full of excited hope, Cambridge voices urgent and with a note of fear as they sought to will forward a runner whose effort they knew to be fading out.

'Come on!' a voice screamed. 'Keep it *up*! Keep *going*!'

The voice was mine. Beside me on the nearer line of the take-over zone Rideout also screamed, encouraging his own colleague.

Both runners coming in were white-faced, with their eyes half-closed, obviously at the end of their resources. Had there been time to think, the sight would not have been a heartening one for men about to embark on the same exercise. In theory the handing over of the baton takes place when the outgoing man has already worked up a fair degree of speed, thus giving him a flying start. The theory can't always be put into practice. The Oxford runner still had a little steam left in him. I felt rather than saw Rideout begin to move away so that his receipt of the baton would take place somewhere inside the zone. It would have been ill-advised for me to go off expecting to be overtaken by my colleague. He had run his heart out. His limbs were locking with fatigue, threatening to bring him to a full stop. Wearily he extended the baton as I waited on the extreme outer edge of the zone. When he handed over he had almost come to a halt. Turning to drive off, I saw that Rideout was several yards ahead.

In a relay race, a substantial lead is a great comfort to the man in front, but a short lead can be a great challenge to the man behind. It wakes in him the need for instant action. There is a target to be aimed at. His partisans are shouting him on. To abolish that lead at once will give a fillip to his own confidence and a sharp blow to his rival's. This was the crucial stage of the relay. At the third take-over the dangerous Pennington was waiting. Should Rideout and I finish on level terms then it was long odds on an Oxford victory, though Palmer would fight his opponent hard. An advantage had to be gained, and it was better to gain it now. The end of the stage was too far away to think whether it might be possible to assert a lead on the run-in. Very likely at the end of a quarter-mile neither the Oxford man nor myself would have any more assertiveness than would just keep us going. The first furlong was the stretch over which to come to a decision.

Expanded, this was how the reasoning would have run. But there was no time for a cool, judicious balancing of pros and cons. Time only for action, instinct only for action. Whether Rideout started off at a reasonable rate for an average, even-paced quarter-mile I don't know. His rival didn't. His rival blazed off flat-out, intent only on abolishing the Oxford lead, intent on establishing a lead for Cambridge, and intent then on keeping it.

Our course was roughly three sides of a square, with a bit of the fourth thrown in. Before the first side was covered, Rideout had been overtaken. Down the second side, which included the hundred yards track – in the previous year so often and so distressfully run over – the engine simply ran away. Power was there. Lots of it. It seemed to have come from nowhere. Power and resolution. The triumphant shouts of Cambridge supporters and the sudden silence of the visitors from Oxford indicated that Rideout had been dropped, and decisively. The thought didn't persuade one to slacken off. Rather did it sharpen resolution. The mind glowed with content.

Legs were beginning to feel a little heavy. Breathing became a little laboured as the lungs strove to take in extra supplies of air. Off the home straight now on to the long curve past the pavilion. Legs were tightening with fatigue. My God, this was a hell of a long way. No wonder quarter-milers looked done up at the end of a race. Excited figures, with coloured scarves wound round their necks, stood on the pavilion steps shrieking and swinging their arms as if seeking to create a wind which would blow one along as far as the third take-over.

Palmer was jiggling his legs excitedly on the near side of the zone. He couldn't be seen very clearly. The pale December sky seemed to be growing dark. Dear God, the weight of the legs, the revulsion of the tortured body from this punishment. Skin and flesh felt rigid now with the accumulation of lactic acid from muscle break-down. These were no longer limbs that were being moved, but in-animate projections, hard and massy as metal. Remote in its eyrie, the mind cared nothing for the plaints of the body. Keep moving, it urged exultantly. Only a few more yards. Keep moving. Cut a decent figure going in. Let's have no nonsense like throwing the head back and thrashing the arms about. That never helps. It wastes less energy if you maintain a steady posture, and it gives your ego a boost, too. So just keep moving.

The last few steps are taken as wearily as if the feet were being plucked out of the suction of a quagmire. But they are completed in good order. The baton is extended. Palmer snatches it and is away. Pennington remains and frets. The lead established on the third stage was nearly twenty yards, too much to be gained back, even though the Oxford anchor man, when he does start, sweeps over the track with great hungry strides. He makes up a deal of the lost ground, but can't make up all. Cambridge supporters shout in triumph as Palmer steams towards the tape. A timekeeper says that he clocked my run unofficially in 49.5 seconds. This is gratifying, but only a small part of the total gratification. The greater part comes from knowledge of something well done, a challenge accepted, a victory deserved.

Having been lost in the outer darkness for some time, one had at last found a way back into the light. A good race had been run this once. Other good races would follow. The mind, a little while ago so uncertain of itself, was now free, confident, and full of appetite for the future.

Molem agitat mens.

Of all the factors that go to make up a runner, the mental factor is far and away the most important. For the mental factor is what drives you to become a runner in the first instance. If that factor should be dulled or blunted, the handicap is almost as serious as the loss of a leg.

Since the war, scientists have shown increasing interest in the physiology of runners – in the functioning of their heart, lungs, nervous system, and so on, and in the mechanics of the body's movements. Experiments have been carried out with subjects on 'treadmills' to determine pulse beat, fatigue accumulation rate, and oxygen requirements under conditions of stress. No doubt this study has advanced the cause of science, and will have been of interest to runners with an enquiring turn of mind, but it cannot be said to have advanced the cause of running much. Science can tell us something of the 'how' of a fact already known, but doesn't make such a big contribution towards discovering the ultimate 'why'. Before Newton, men knew that an apple detaching itself from the bough of a tree would fall to the ground. The law of gravity demonstrated the force behind this fact, but did nothing to prevent future apples from hitting the ground.

Thus for a scientist to record the observation that the pulse of a great runner at rest registers 40 beats instead of the normal 80 may be a matter of moment, but it doesn't explain why that runner has developed his heart muscles over many years by strenuous exercise to the point where they are able to do a greater amount of work in the matter of pumping blood round the body, or do that work more easily, than can the heart-muscles of a non-runner.

Science also reveals that lactic acid is the most deleterious of the fatigue products accumulated in the body as a result of muscle break-down under stress, and concludes that the runner with the highest tolerance of lactic acid is likely to run farthest. But the runner already knew this before the scientist came along with his stethoscope and his manometer and his other gadgets. The runner knew that his legs became heavy with fatigue if he made a prolonged effort. It mattered little to him whether the substance causing the heaviness was lactic acid or bicarbonate of soda. He also knew that he would be able to endure this heaviness longer in competition if he got himself into the habit of enduring it in training.

Science will explain a runner, or it will explain part of him. It will never make a runner. Only the man's own mind can do that, deliberately choosing the way and then resolutely following it.

The choice, and the resolution, will determine a runner's success more than his physical attributes. The first commodity a salesman has to sell is himself, and the first person he sells it to is himself. A runner is in the same position. If he has no faith or belief in what he is doing, he will be a frequently-defeated runner. If he does believe, his defeats at first may be almost as frequent, but as time goes on they will decrease in number. If he strives his utmost to avoid being beaten, or rather, if he strives with the firm intention of winning, his determination is bound to tell in the end.

Resolution is the basic factor. If one can be intelligent as well, it is an advantage, especially in racing above the sprint distances. Not only bodies compete in running, but also wills. Often the stronger will can defeat the theoretically stronger body. One has seen it happen time and again, the way a clever runner will play an opponent like a fish, trying to upset him and harass him out of the normal mode of his performance. If the opponent likes a slow pace to be set at first, the clever rival will set him a fast one. If the opponent prefers not to lead, but to win his races from behind, the rival will try to lure him into a position where he has to go out in front. If the opponent prefers even-paced running, the rival will try to break him up with sudden changes of speed. Yet while the one man is trying to conquer the other by establishing a moral ascendancy over him, danger exists that he will break himself up in the process. Danger also exists that the opponent, proving cleverer and more determined than had been expected, will play some disturbing tricks of his own.

If any race can be said to have been won by sheer resolution, it must be the 5,000 metres contest between C. J. Chataway and V. Kuts at London's White City stadium in October 1954. Two months previously, in the European Games held at Berne, Kuts, a comparatively unknown Russian, had beaten the British champion by a humiliating distance. The defeat surprised Chataway, who until then had regarded E. Zatopek of Czecho-Slovakia as his chief rival over 5,000 metres, and it was a shock to the British sporting public, who had got into the habit of thinking Chataway invincible.

The athletics match between Britain and the U.S.S.R., in which the two men were to meet once more, aroused the greatest interest. Nothing was more certain than that Kuts, a man who carried out an iron training programme, would seek to repeat his victory of Berne and thus stamp himself without question as the British runner's master. It was no less certain that Chataway would be eager to avenge his earlier humiliation, and especially eager to do so in front of his own compatriots.

Morally, Chataway was at a disadvantage. He had been beaten once, and decisively, by this Russian. Another swingeing defeat might well crack his confidence. Further, Kuts had the strength of mind to win his races from in front, to break his opponents by mounting sudden and frequent bursts of speed. Until now Chataway had run his own 3 miles or 5,000 metres courses at a fairly even pace, relying on a driving finish over the last lap to pull away from the rest of the field. But no one who stuck close to Kuts could expect to run at an even pace, nor was he likely to have much energy left for a finishing drive. This race was going to be a war both of nerves and of bodily attrition. Chataway had the disagreeable knowledge that his opponent was going to dictate the contest, and that he had to answer the dictation.

Not only the runners suffered in that race, but also every person watching, whether present in the stadium or sitting in front of a television screen. Rarely can an athlete have had such moral support lavished on him as Chataway did. He needed it. In the course of the Berne 5,000 metres Kuts had set up a new world record. His lap times at the White City showed that he was going to run this race yet faster. The man radiated strength and determination. After the first four laps, there were only two runners in it, the British and Russian second strings having been dropped. Almost every lap, along the back straight, Kuts drove himself into a sprint, desperately trying to shake off the red-haired Briton behind him. Chataway refused to be shaken. This was what Kuts had done at Berne. He mustn't be allowed to do it again. But the physical agony, both of the Russian trying to break away and of the Briton refusing to let him, was cruel. It couldn't only be seen by the spectators. It could be *felt*.

The closing stages of the race were run in a pandemonium of noise which rocked the concrete walls of the stadium. Men shrieked hoarsely and nonsensically, beating their fists on each other's shoulders. Women wept and put their hands up, veiling their eyes from the torture taking place down on the quarter-mile oval. How flesh and blood could stand it, no one knew. This was a battle of giants, such as might never be seen again. A battle of two heroes, out by themselves in an intolerable loneliness, each grimly determined on only one thing, not to show weakness in face of the other's strength.

By the time the spotlight came on to them for the last lap, neither can have been much aware of his surroundings. They had long gone past the stage of mere physical exhaustion. Nothing more than will-power, and the last reserves of courage and spirit, kept them going. Throughout the whole race there had never been a gap between them of more than a yard or two. There was the same gap now. No question of either man raising a finishing sprint. The power had been drained from them both. A miracle that they were still moving in good order, the suffering visible in their faces but hardly at all in their arms and leg movements.

Every single spectator in the stadium had gone mad. The runners were on the crown of the final bend now, almost close enough to touch each other. And the spectators were with them. Only in the flesh did they remain on the terraces. In the spirit they were down on that blood-red track, on that finishing straight, on that final run-in to the tape. And they knew that their man had been exhausted. They knew it was impossible for Chataway to find the

155

strength to overtake this iron Russian. More than three miles of hell had ground him into the track.

But, by God, Chataway *was* coming up! He had moved out from behind Kuts. He still had an effort left in him after this awful savaging! Both runners were reeling. Their progress towards the tape seemed to take place in slow motion. Kuts realised that the impossible was happening, that he was being challenged by a rival who should, on form, have been killed off. He couldn't respond to the challenge. His head went back as he sought to draw yet further on his reserves. But no reserves were left. Chataway was at his shoulder. Where that ultimate spurt of energy came from, no one will ever know. Sufficient that it came. It transmitted a final drive to muscles seized with fatigue. There was never any surrender by Kuts, but only the victory of one great heart over another by a mere fraction. In such a thunder of sound that it seemed incredible the stadium could remain standing, Chataway broke the tape two feet ahead of his rival.

Mentem agitat mens.

The mind is not only a spur to the body, but also to itself. It can overcome the insuperable barriers of its own raising.

The vision of a four minute mile was something dreamt of long before 1954. Paavo Nurmi of Finland was probably the first to give it serious consideration when he declared that it might be done by an athlete whose judgment of pace was so accurate that he could run four quarter-mile laps of 60 seconds each. But Nurmi's great days were in the nineteen-twenties. Times for the mile were steadily reduced during the years before the outbreak of the Second World War. During the war the Swedes, A. Andersson and G. Haegg, very nearly approached four minutes but never quite reached it. They did this so often that it began to seem the figure was unattainable.

Time passed after the war. As men like W. Lueg, W. Santee, J. L. Landy and R. G. Bannister made attack after unavailing attack on the objective, opinion began to harden in certain quarters that they were attempting the impossible. And once the notion is well advertised that a thing is impossible, it will become impossible. Men will approach the task not believing in their competence to perform it. A barrier will have been raised, not a physical obstacle but a mental one. Conquering such a barrier requires an extraordinary degree of faith on the part of the conqueror. That is the real measure of Bannister's achievement when he finally broke through in 1954. The physical effort needed was considerable, but it was much harder to keep a mind undaunted in the face of pessimism and disbelief.

Once the barrier had been scaled, the effect was immediately apparent. Knowing now that a mile could be run in less than four minutes, other men went ahead and did so. To date, some twenty athletes have performed the exercise a matter of fifty times. But they have done it with Bannister's help. He did it on his own.

Robert Mills had an experience which bears on the same point. Mills was a high jumper, six feet two inches tall, with long, thin legs and arms. Like many of his calling, except in the number of limbs, he looked a bit of a spider.

Until 1957, Mills had never managed to top 6 feet 2 inches in his jumping, exactly his own height, that is. So regularly did he fail when the bar was set any higher that at last he convinced himself he had reached his maximum. Up to 6 feet 2 inches he vaulted confidently and with a smooth, clear-cut technique. An inch beyond that and both confidence and technique deserted him. Making his run-up

157

across the fan one could see that the spark just wasn't in him. His coach pleaded with him, arguing that a man should be able to jump well above his own height, trying to inject that dose of belief which would make Mills rise above his present level. But the jumper's mind was too set and fixed in his obsession. He failed because he knew he was going to fail.

In 1957 the controversy over the built-up shoe broke out. With this aid, of doubtful legality, the Russians began to jump towering heights. High jumpers in other parts of the world were interested in the development. Mills's coach persuaded him to see what he could do with the device, merely out of curiosity, he said. Mills put a built-up shoe on his jumping foot, and tried it out. He did so casually, for a lark, not bothering to make his usual calculated approach across the fan. He cleared 6 feet 3 inches. Thoughtful, he watched while the coach put the bar up another half-inch. He cleared that height, too, though his approach was less casual this time. Within a week, the high jumper had reached the very good height of 6 feet 5½ inches.

After he had done so, the coach put the bar a fraction lower.

'Now,' he said, 'take off that built-up shoe and make an attempt in your ordinary shoes.'

'But that's silly,' Mills protested. 'It's only because of the shoe that I've been able to get up as far as that.'

'Are you sure?'

'Of course. Normally I've never done better than six two.'

'The fact remains that, normally or abnormally, you've just cleared six five and a half. You have actually been up to that height. I say you can get up to it again!'

Mills did, or he got within half an inch of it. In his ordinary jumping shoes, with no benefit of sole inch or inch and a half thick, he cleared 6 feet 5 inches, three inches better than what he had previously believed to be his maximum. He cleared it because now he knew he was capable of clearing it.

A man runs with his legs, but he also runs with his head and his heart. He has to get his body fit, but he has also to know himself and his opponents and the general context of his sport. More than anything, he must feel that pleasurable confidence in running, that surge of spirit which makes him want to compete and want to do his best. Always he should be out to win, even when he is pitted against opposition so formidable that the chances of winning are pretty remote. Defeat should not depress him but should make him angry, put him on his mettle, make him determine to strive with even greater effort next time. By trial and error he will find his level of competence, and as soon as it is found he will want to go beyond it. If the mental spearhead is kept sharp and bright, then going beyond it will not prove too difficult, nor going beyond the next level which he sees rising before him. Steps were made to be climbed.

The run in the 4 x 440 relay against Oxford sharpened the spearhead for me, with no more delay than if a knife had been put to a grindstone. Outlook on running changed unbelievably. One hadn't, after all, fallen into the gulf which separates the promise of ignorant youth from the more solid, knowledgeable performance of manhood. Two years had been consumed in discovering the fact, but there was still time left in which to apply it. One could start building again at the point where building operations seemed to have stopped for good in the summer of 1935.

Even the weather seemed to improve, to become sunnier and brighter. Probably it didn't in fact, but in memory at any rate the second two years at Fenner's were a time of perpetual spring, whereas the first two had been dark with winter. Training ceased to be an irksome chore. The hundred yards track, bounded on the one side by white posts and rails and on the other by the grass of the cricket pitch, was no longer a grudging enemy but a somewhat wayward friend. Wayward because of that infernal, strength-sapping south-west wind into the eye of which we so often ran. But even the wind couldn't stop the running from being enjoyable, from being an affair of pleasure instead of a harsh, toilsome struggle. Defeats in the running still came, but they weren't defeats one had reconciled oneself to before a race ever started. And there were victories over men of some renown to compensate for the defeats. The giants with whom we came into contact at Fenner's were at last cut down to the size of ordinary human beings.

One of the C.U.A.C.'s regular fixtures was with a team matched against us by the A.A.A. in the Easter term. Our opponents were usually quite strong, for the A.A.A. does not care to have its champions beaten on such occasions. In two successive such meetings I found myself up against A. W. Sweeney in both the hundred yards and the furlong. Sweeney was the best British sprinter of the day, and had been a member of the U.K. team that went to Berlin for the Olympic Games. On both occasions Sweeney beat me in the hundred yards, the first time by a clear yard and the second time by two feet. The results were as commonly expected. That I should have dealt with the A.A.A. second string in the two races was some cause for satisfaction, but not enough. It would have been much greater cause to have dealt with the first string.

The race over two-twenty yards in the first match did not go as commonly expected. Here, the difference in outlook from a year ago was marked. A year ago, in such a meeting, I would have been put off by the reputation of the big name. A defeat by him in the short sprint would have confirmed the off-putting when the time came for the furlong. Now it didn't.

The furlong wasn't a race commonly run at Fenner's since the event did not then form part of the programme for the Sports against Oxford. When such a race was staged, it took place over a dog-leg course which the innocent visitor, accustomed to the standard quarter-mile oval, often found disconcerting. We started on the far side of the track, under the red brick walls of Homerton Training College, from the windows of which young women gazed down disdainfully at the childish antics of grown men. A fifty-yards straight took us from the start into a very sharp, right-angled bend, out of which we emerged into the final straight of a hundred and fifty yards. That final straight was a killer, above all if a steady wind blew in your teeth. Only a few degrees less perilous was the bend. It came precisely at that point in a furlong where the sprinter is still going flat out, before he has eased off ever so slightly into that mid-stream coast, from which he will build up into his final effort. Try going into a sharp, right-angled bend some time when you're running at around evens pace. It's an interesting experience. You feel like a tram that's jumped off the rails.

We, who had knowledge of the bend, leaned into it, literally, counter-balancing hard like a motor-cyclist fighting against centrifugal force. In the furlong race of the first match Sweeney and his A.A.A. team-mate had no knowledge of the bend. It yawned in front of them suddenly like a pit dug for tigers. If they hadn't braked violently they'd have sped across the top of the final straight and crashed through the fence into the University Lawn Tennis Club courts, perhaps to the detriment of some tense rally.

So, braking and lurching, Sweeney negotiated the bend. By the time he got back on an even keel he found he was several yards down on me. Gathering his wits after the harassing experience he pulled back some of the yards, but he couldn't pull back all. Afterwards he smiled pleasantly through his R.A.F. handle-bar moustache and he said he would lay down a special 220 yards track of his own some time and invite me to compete on it.

In the first match against the A.A.A. the credit for defeating Sweeney had to be given to the Fenner's bend, but I take some of the credit for the second defeat. That time Sweeney was ready for the bend. He took a good look at it. He did a trial run round it. He'd also taken a good look at me and was in no mood to notch another failure against the C.U.A.C. at this distance. I drew the inside lane, with him in number 2, but the stagger was so small, owing to the peculiar shape of the course, that there was little advantage in the position. Except that to have Sweeney in front of me, to the left (we ran right-hand inside) was a spur.

Sometimes, in a furlong, there was a temptation not to go off too hard, to keep a good head of steam for that grinding 150-yards straight. This was no occasion for half-measures. This was an occasion for opening the throttle wide right from the gun, and keeping it open. Once a sprinter of Sweeney's calibre was allowed to establish a lead there would be no hope of cutting it back. He had to be fought relentlessly all the way, otherwise one might as well admit defeat at the start.

It was a fight, too. Going into the bend with the first fifty-yards straight behind us we were level. Coming out of the bend Sweeney had momentarily disappeared. Perhaps I had gained a yard on him. But a mere fraction of a second later he had come back into view. I could see him out of the corner of my left eye. He was astern, but by very little, no more than a couple of feet and maybe less. Ahead of us stretched one hundred and fifty mortal yards. In such a distance a two foot deficit could easily be made up. It could easily be converted into a commanding lead.

I thought that race would never end. A boundless grey cinder desert seemed to lie in front of me. The finish was so far away that it simply had no relevance. Shouts of encouragement came from somewhere, but for what or for whom I had no time to think. My mind was exclusively occupied with the figure at my left shoulder, and the fear which it engendered. The figure had to be kept off. At all costs the figure had to be kept off. No chance here for a midstream coast which, while it consumes less energy, allows almost full speed to be maintained. He was straining to get at me, therefore I must strain to keep away from him. The throttle was kept wide open the whole time, regardless of how steam pressure might drop in the boiler.

And the pressure was dropping. No doubt of that. Leg movements were becoming heavy. Breath hissed as the lungs sucked it in. Would that finish never come? Would the limbs tie up first? But however the body felt, the mind remained keen and urgent. That figure was still at the left shoulder, still slightly astern, probably by no more than a foot now. More power, said the mind. No power left, said the legs. There's got to be, said the mind. He's as tired as you are. He isn't coming up any more. Your lead is sticking at a foot. Only thirty yards to go now. Only thirty yards to the tape. You've practically made it. Only if you break down can he beat you. The pair of you are running stride for stride, taking breath for breath, your faces twisted in agony, both reaching desperately for that tape.

But you're a foot in front, so you reach it first.

Possibly the furlong would have been a better distance to concentrate on. Probably, if it had at that time been included among the events for the Varsity Sports, I would have concentrated on it. But having started off as a sprinter over the short distance, and being mainly called upon for that distance, recognition of competence had to be sought there.

And, to have your competence as a hundred yards man recognised, you must return evens.

The quest for evens had begun in 1935. During the two intervening years it looked as if it had foundered. Now it could be resumed, with less youthful exuberance but more mature knowledge. The quest lasted some time, so that the steadier attitude towards it was a great help.

In 1938 I ran as first string in the 100 yards for Cambridge at the Varsity Sports. Pennington ran as first string for Oxford. The experts thought that whoever won it would have to return 10 seconds to do so. They were quite right. Pennington edged me into second place and the time-keepers gave him what I would have dearly liked to have had myself. There is something about the announcement when it comes over the loudspeakers. 'Ten seconds.' Short and clipped, just like that. No laborious mucking about with decimal points, but the statement of a solid, workman-like job, the performance of a runner who's mastered his craft. What my own time was in the race I didn't learn. Before the war they rarely bothered to give the details of a placed runner's performance. It must have been around the evens mark, but it wasn't recorded and therefore I could take no credit for it. The quest had to continue.

For nearly another year I chased evens, until the goal became as elusive as the end of a rainbow. Every time I turned out in a hundred, I turned out with one object in mind, to get rid of the decimal points. But they stuck as obstinately as fly-paper sticks to a fly. Ten point two, ten point one, ten point three, ten point one. Considering the unfavourable wintry conditions in which we often ran, these times were not bad, but when a time is put down in the record book the conditions aren't recorded as well. Ten point one returned on a snow-bound track in January still rates lower than ten seconds returned on a warm still summer's day. There's a yard difference in speed. You have to get rid of that yard. Where or when you get rid of it does not concern the record books.

Our regular time-keeper at Fenner's was F. N. Drake-Digby. He had a reputation for being severe with the watch, especially where it was a question of a good time being allowed. Men said that for 'Drake' to give you evens you'd probably have to do better than 9.95. Certainly, they said, if you returned the bare ten he would announce it as ten point one. When we challenged 'Drake' himself on the point he smiled and said nothing.

Officials of Drake-Digby's status had to be careful. They were time-keepers appointed by the A.A.A. On the verdicts of their watches, records might depend. Any times they announced had to be genuine, unimpeachable, not liable to crack under critical examination. If they erred on the side of severity, it was in a good cause.

But we, who ran, did not always appreciate the good cause.

At the end of what we thought was a fast hundred, we would approach him.

'Come on, "Drake",' we would urge, 'that was ten. Ten point nought one, at the worst. Come on, do the decent thing for once.'

Drake-Digby would look at the watch, slip it back into his pocket, stick his cigarette holder out of his mouth at a defiant angle, and pronounce judgment.

'Ten point one.'

And so the moving finger would write off yet another attempt at evens. It wrote off so many of them that one lost count. The failures might have been cause for despair. Recognition of full competence as a sprinter seemed as far away as ever. But hope did not flag.

If I was to do evens, I wanted to do it first on the Fenner's ground. That was the ground with which most of my running had been associated to date, and, as it turned out, the ground with which most of my running was associated, period. 1939 was not a year in which to make extensive plans for future running.

In March we were still unaware of that fact. In March the University Sports were held at Fenner's prior to the match against Oxford at the White City. It was my last chance of winning a hundred yards in evens on the ground where I had known much gloom and much happiness.

For once, the conditions were right. Despite the early season of the year, the weather was mild. If any wind blew up the track it was a mere gentle breeze, and not a half gale. The track was firm. I had the feeling a runner has when he knows he's going to run a good race, outwardly a little nervous but inwardly relaxed, with the motor ticking over gently and ready to respond at once to any pressure on the accelerator. The race seemed to go very smoothly, and with surprisingly little effort. From the gun I felt myself moving away, until the other white-vested, white-shorted figures were lost sight of. Up at the tape it was quite lonely.

I sought out the time-keeper. If that wasn't a good race, then my judgment of running was so far at fault that I'd better give it up.

'Well, "Drake", have I done it?'

Drake-Digby looked at his watch, slipped it into his pocket, stuck his cigarette holder out of his mouth at an angle, and nodded.

'Ten seconds,' he said.

Two words, and they justified years of effort and strain and sacrifice and unhappiness. Two words which were a certificate of competence as a sprinter, a late but authori-

tive endorsement of promise shown what now seemed
ke a long time ago. I had first entered this ground with
travagant hopes. Now I was leaving it with more sober
nfidence.

Evens is the sprinter's first important milestone. To break
ens is the second.

In July of the same year was held one of the last first-class
ack meetings in which either I or anyone else would com-
ete for the next six years – the inter-club contest for the
addilove Trophy held at the Birchfield Harriers ground
Birmingham. As a member of the Achilles Club team I
n in the hundred yards and the medley relay. The field
r the hundred yards was strong, with a number of even-
ners among the competitors. H. C. Wickerson promised
be the most dangerous.

We ran heats and a final. Wickerson won his heat in
.1 seconds. I won mine in 10 seconds. The sound of the
vo short words coming over the amplifiers was a melody,
id a challenge to the opposition. It seemed pretty clear that
hoever won the final would have to break evens to do so.

The thought suddenly exploded in the brain. To break
ens! It was an ambition, certainly, but hadn't been
nong the possibilities envisaged today. One had imagined
more as a target for next season. But it might not be next
ason. It might be here and now. These chances often
me unexpectedly. You had to take them when they
fered. Unless a man was a blindingly fast mover he
dn't often break evens without good opposition to push
m. That opposition was certainly present this afternoon.
The trial had taken you unawares, but you had grown
t of that state of mind where the unexpected threw you
f balance. This was going to be a fast race. Good. Wicker-
n was a first-class man, an international. Excellent. He
uld be all out to win. So would others. Don't you think

you shot your bolt in the heat? Absolutely not. Weren
you worried in case you didn't measure up to this strenuo
challenge? Far from it.

Holes were dug. Track suits were stripped off. T
starter loaded his guns. The familiar words rang out.

'Get to your marks!'

How many times had you heard them? How many tim
had you waited for them with nervous excitement flowin
in you like an electric current? And then felt the exciteme
begin to die down as you went forward soberly to yo
holes, knowing that this was the moment of truth?

The turf was springy under your right knee, your fe
fitted snugly into their supports, your muscles were war
and supple. On either side of you the others were fidgetin
getting themselves settled. The crowd noises hushe
Everyone seemed to be holding their breath.

'Get set!'

Your body was wound up like a spring now, waiting f
release. Right foot would thrust against the back hole, le
foot pull on the front, arms would break into their powerf
semi-rotary drive. You concentrated on the strip of gra
in front of you, head down, imagining that first stride, se
ing where it would hit, willing it to be fast and powerfu
desperate to hurtle straight and true down the chal
marked lane.

The gun!

You had gone. It was a good start. Your movements fe
easy. Without conscious body adjustment you had con
up from the crouching to the sprinting attitude. The win
created by your own passage through the air was singin
past your ears. But others had also started well. This wa
a top-grade race. On your right a faint grey shadow. O
your left a faint grey shadow. From the degree of definitic
of the shadows experience reckoned the two rivals wei

more or less level with you. Halfway, and the shadows were still there. This race was between the three of you. Your eyes were on the tape, willing it to come faster towards you. You felt that sense of ever-increasing acceleration which may be illusory but is always comforting, because it means you are making your full effort, and without strain.

By God, the shadow on the left was fading a little! But the shadow on the right was growing a little clearer! Time for a last effort, a last lunge towards the post. Too late. There were only inches in it but you knew he'd beaten you. For when the worsted came across your chest the tension had been snapped out of it. You had lost, but it had been a good race, a race faster than your heat.

'First, Wickerson,' an official read out. 'Second, Loader. Third, Hampshire. Winner's time, 9.9 seconds.'

You walked over to the time-keepers. The time returned by the second man would not be announced officially.

'Can you tell me what I did?'

'Same time,' they nodded. '9.9 seconds.'

When a thing is well done, you know it. Listen to the 'bell-note' which comes when eight oars, struck into the water, take hold of it in unison. Listen to the full-blooded thwack as a golf ball is driven straight and true from the tee. Look and listen as a first-class batsman on top of his form makes a cover drive. The bat has been swung in the correct arc, the weight of the body is correctly distributed and its direction correctly angled, the ball is struck at the correct time and with the correct force, the correct allowance having been made for any spin imparted by hand or pitch. The result is a deep-toned boom of the bat as if a cannon had roared. You do not need to look, probably the ball is going so fast that you cannot look. That shot was a boundary from the moment the ball left the bowler's hand.

Thus also with running. The sprinter knows when he is doing even time. He hardly needs the assurance of the watch on the point. The ease, the apparent lack of effort with which he moves, inform him. A number of lines of force have become concentrated in an apex, and the apex is a spearhead, driving him along. Conscious thought plays little part in his effort, for thinking did its work in the past, when the long routine of training had to be endured. Now there is only the instinct for action, with the urge from inside and the stimulus of rivalry from outside combining to drive him along.

Motion is light and fluid, trammelled by no barriers. Limbs thrust, press, recover, thrust, in a cycle of movement so smooth as to be almost mechanical. The runner feels his own wind on his face. If he looked at the ground it would be a blur, but he doesn't look at the ground, he looks at the tape, feeling it draw him like a lodestone. His body is being carried forward with a swiftsure speed so easy that he is hardly conscious of speed. The track does not seem to be traversed by individual, separate steps deliberately taken by flesh and blood but rather by a surging flow of spirit. The man feels suspended in mid-air, swept along by some irresistible force.

Such is the exhilaration of the hundred yards dash, the utmost trial of speed that the human frame can make. No long endurance this, but a sword thrust, an arrow's flight, a flash so quick that the human eye must follow it in jerks and not in a steady sweep of vision. Ten seconds ago the athlete was still crouched at the start, waiting for the pistol shot. Now his chest is snapping the worsted. Strength, energy, resolution, have been perfectly applied to the task in hand.

At such a moment there is no need for anyone to tell you. You know you can run. I mean, really run.